ENGLISH

英语核心素养下的本土文化教学

主　编 / 李细娟
副主编 / 谭玉琳　余优玲
陈娟丽

东北师范大学出版社
长　春

图书在版编目（CIP）数据

英语核心素养下的本土文化教学 / 李细娟主编. —长春：东北师范大学出版社，2021.11

ISBN 978-7-5681-7537-1

Ⅰ. ①英… Ⅱ. ①李… Ⅲ. ①英语课—教学研究—中学 Ⅳ. ①G633.412

中国版本图书馆CIP数据核字（2021）第219489号

□责任编辑：石　斌　　□封面设计：言之凿
□责任校对：刘彦妮　张小娅　□责任印制：许　冰

东北师范大学出版社出版发行
长春净月经济开发区金宝街 118 号（邮政编码：130117）
电话：0431-84568023
网址：http：//www.nenup.com
北京言之凿文化发展有限公司设计部制版
北京政采印刷服务有限公司印装
北京市中关村科技园区通州园金桥科技产业基地环科中路 17 号（邮编：101102）
2022年4月第1版　2022年4月第1次印刷
幅面尺寸：170mm × 240mm　印张：9.5　字数：140千

定价：45.00元

前言

FOREWORD

新丰县地处广东省中部偏北、韶关市南端、珠三角发达经济圈边缘，南连从化、龙门，北接翁源，东邻连平，西靠佛冈，与广州、深圳、东莞、佛山等珠三角城市的距离均在200千米半径范围内，是韶关承接沿海产业转移的前沿阵地。

新丰县在南齐武帝永明元年（483年）建制，取“物产丰富”之意，属广州南海郡。此后，曾用休吉、长宁等县名，先后隶属循州、龙川、惠州、广州等，1988年1月划归韶关市管辖至今。新丰县人文底蕴深厚，历史上出现了许多杰出人士，有宋初岭南进士第一人古成之、明朝吏部天官姚钿、黄埔军校第一期毕业生潘学吟、红军早期领导人李任予、见义勇为英雄张桂扬等。

文化意识指对中外文化的理解和对优秀文化的认同，文化意识体现英语学科核心素养的价值取向。文化意识的培养有助于学生增强国家认同和家国情怀，坚定文化自信，树立人类命运共同体意识，学会做人做事。本书以立足学生发展的英语学科核心素养为导向，以新丰文化为载体，以用英语推广新丰文化为目标，旨在让读者了解新丰文化，培养文化意识和文化自信，并辩证地看待新丰文化以及创新性地传承和发扬新丰文化，传播中华文化。

目录

CONTENTS

第一辑

校本课程

Unit 1 Brief Introduction to Xinfeng

1.1 Listening and Speaking: Welcome to Xinfeng

(1) Listen to a song: *Welcome to Xinfeng*

Welcome to Xinfeng

Lyrics by：Chen Bo, Xie Yi

Composed by：Liu Xiang

Sung by：Wan Li

(Chorus)

If you happen to be free, welcome to Xinfeng

I will be waiting for you in Yunji Mountain, till the mountain is covered with red maple leaves

If you happen to be free, welcome to Xinfeng

I will be waiting for you in Swallow Grotto, hoping to watch the rainbow with you

(Chorus) Welcome to Xinfeng

(Chorus) Happiness will be around you every minute

(Chorus) Welcome to Xinfeng

(Chorus) We shall meet with relaxing songs and sweet smiles

Xinfeng River and majestic mountain scenery speak their romance

Yuntianhai Hot Spring embraces you in a tender way

By Xianren Grinding Stone and Bamboo Forest Fountain, flowers grow thick, people pray heartedly

Along with the seasonal view and clear sky, Oriental Cherry Valley shows different faces

Under Xiutian Ancient Tree and by Lugu River bank, Xinfeng welcomes guests from all over the world

(2) Describe Xinfeng according to the mind map given below

population

location

food

attractions

famous figures

latest development

1.2 Reading 1

A Brief Introduction to Xinfeng

Monday 1st October, 2018

As we **got tired of** the busy life in Guangzhou, my husband John and I decided to **join in** a 7-day trip to Xinfeng during the National Day holiday. **It was the first time that we had been** to Xinfeng, a county of about 2,015 square kilometers, but with a population of only about 262,000. **While driving there**, we hoped that we could **no longer suffer** the great stress from work. Thanks to the **highway**, it only took us one and a half hours to drive to Xinfeng County, which is about 150 kilometers away from

Guangzhou.

On arriving there, John's friend Tom entertained ① us and introduced us to a lot of famous attractions, **such as** Yunji Mountain, Yunji Ancient Town, Xilian Mountain, Oriental Cherry Valley, ② the national-level wetland park Lugu River Natural Reserve ③ and so on. We couldn't wait to witness their wonderful **views**, so we drove directly to our first stop-an old-growth forest resort ④ named "Yuntianhai Hot Spring" in Meikeng Town. On the way there, Tom told us that because of its beautiful environment, Xinfeng was honored as "the important ecological ⑤ protective screen of Guangdong" and "the national key ecological functi area". The amazing scenery on both sides **kept us spellbound**, so we didn't even notice that we had arrived.

I found that this most beautiful hot spring resort in Guangdong was surrounded by mountains and with lush ⑥ woods in it. The staff there also told us it was known as a "natural air anion bar" ⑦. We **did make** the right choice for the first stop. After experiencing the relaxing hot spring, we completely forgot the troubles that we **were upset about**. Therefore, we **determined** to visit the rest five towns and streets in the following six days.

1.3 Reading 2

A Brief Introduction to Yan Tower of Xinfeng

Tuesday 2nd October, 2018

---

① entertain *v.* 招待。

② Oriental Cherry Valley 樱花峪。

③ Natural Reserve 自然保护区。

④ resort *n.*度假村。

⑤ ecological *adj.* 生态的。

⑥ lush *adj.* 茂盛的。

⑦ natural air anion bar 天然氧吧；anion *n.*负离子。

Today was our second day in Xinfeng, and Tom took us to go hiking **outdoors**. We headed for the Yan Tower Park **which** is located in Fengcheng Town. Because I believed doing sports was a way to relax myself, I felt extremely excited about that.

Luckily, a professional local guide introduced the park to us in detail today, so we learned **a series of** knowledge about Yan Tower.

Yan Tower was located on top of the Laowei Mountain, formerly known as Shuangfeng Mountain. According to the records of *Xinfeng Historical Annals*[①], it was Chen Zhangyi, the magistrate[②] of Changning County, **who** proposed[③] to build Yan Tower in 1739. The tour guide also introduced that Yan Tower was a famous tourist attraction[④] in Ming and Qing dynasties[⑤] in Xinfeng County, as well as a cultural relic protection site[⑥] in Guangdong Province.

Its appearance was **so unique that** we couldn't ignore it. The hexagonal[⑦] tower had 13 wooden floors inside leading direct to the top floor. However, looking outside, it **was made up** of seven floors in total. The guide said **because of** its unique structure and ancient style in the mountains, it had certain reference value[⑧] for the study of ancient buildings. When we reached the top, we could enjoy the **entire** scenery of Xinfeng County.

In order to remember these wonderful moments, we took **a number of** photos inside and outside the tower. **At dusk**, we went to the next attraction after **expressing** our **sincere** gratitude to the guide **face to face**.

---

① *Xinfeng Historical Annals*《新丰史志》。

② magistrate *n*. 知县。

③ propose *v*.提议。

④ tourist attraction 景点。

⑤ dynasty *n*. 朝代。

⑥ cultural relic protection site 文物保护遗址。

⑦ hexagonal *adj*. 六角形的。

⑧ reference value 参考价值。

1.4 Writing: A Letter of Invitation

假设你是李华，今年暑假你打算邀请美国朋友Ben和Lisa来新丰度假。请根据下面的要点写一封邀请信给Ben。

1. 来新丰度假一周。

2. 你已经安排好了行程（旅游景点），肖红负责预订航班和酒店。

3. 周四之前回复是否过来。

注意：

1.词数：100左右。

2. 可以适当增加细节，以使行文连贯。

3.信的开头和结尾已为你写好（不计入总词数）。

Dear Ben,

How is everything going? ______________________________

____

____

____

____

____

____

____

____

____

____

____

I am looking forward to your reply.

Yours,

Li Hua

附翻译：

第一单元　新丰概况介绍

1.1 Listening and Speaking

以《请你来新丰》这首歌为引入，借助思维导图讨论新丰概况。

请你来新丰

作词：陈 波　谢 怡　作曲：刘 翔　演唱：万 莉

如果你正好有空　　请你来新丰
我在云髻山等着你　　等到枫叶满山红

如果你正好有空　　请你来新丰
我在燕子岩等着你　　陪你一起看彩虹

哎格依溜哇哟吹咧　　请你来新丰
哎格依溜哇哟吹咧　　幸福相伴每一分钟
哎格依溜哇哟吹咧　　请你来新丰
哎格依溜哇哟吹咧　　欢歌笑语喜相逢
丰江山画浪漫情怀　　云天海里你最懂
仙人磨石竹林泉边　　禅心祈福花生浓
春花秋月天高云淡　　樱花峪里情万种
秀田古树鲁古河畔　　笑迎东西南北中

1.2 Reading 1

新丰概况介绍

2018年10月1日，星期一

因为我们都厌倦了广州忙碌的生活，我跟我的丈夫约翰决定在国庆期间参加一次为期7天的新丰之旅。这是我们第一次到新丰县，这个县总面积大约2000平方千米，但总人口只有约26.2万。开车到那的时候，我们期待着不用再忍受来自工作的巨大压力。多亏了高速公路，我们只花了一个半小时就从广州到达了150千米外的新丰县城。

一到达那里，约翰的朋友汤姆接待了我们，并向我们介绍了很多著名景点，如云髻山、云髻古镇、西莲山、樱花峪和国家级湿地公园鲁古河自然保护区等。我们迫不及待地想一睹这些美景，所以我们直接驾车前往第一站——梅坑镇的云天海温泉原始森林度假村。在去那的路上，汤姆告诉我们，因为其环境优美，新丰被授予“广东重要的生态屏障”和“国家重点生态功能区”等美誉。我们都沉迷于路边美丽的风景，不知不觉便到了。

我发现度假村四面环山，区域内林木繁茂，是广东最美的温泉度假村。那里的工作人员告诉我们云天海被誉为“天然氧吧”。我们果真没选错第一站。在体验了令人放松的温泉后，我们已全然忘却那些让我们感到不安的烦恼。于是，我们决定在接下来的6天游完剩下的5个镇和丰城街道。

1.3 Reading 2

新丰雁塔介绍

2018年10月2日，星期二

今天是我们在新丰的第二天，汤姆带我们到户外徒步旅行。我们前往位于丰城镇的雁塔公园。因为我认为做运动是一种放松的方式，所以我对此感到十分兴奋。

幸运的是，今天有一位很专业的当地导游为我们介绍雁塔，所以我们学到了一系列关于雁塔的知识。

雁塔位于老围山上（古称双凤山）。据《新丰史志》记载，1739年长宁知县陈张翼提议兴建雁塔的。导游还说雁塔是新丰县城著名的明清游览胜地，是广东省的文物保护遗址。

它的外观如此独特，以至于我们无法忽视它。六角形的塔内分十三层木板楼，直通顶层。然而，从外观看，总共由七层组成。导游告诉我们，因为雁塔构造别具一格，有山区古建筑的风貌，所以对研究古建筑有一定的参考价值。当我们登顶时，新丰县城风光一览无遗。

为了留住这些美好的时刻，我们在塔里塔外都拍了很多照片。黄昏时刻，我们当面向导游表达了我们真挚的感谢，便前往下一个景点了。

1.4 Writing：邀请信

附参考范文：

Dear Ben,

How is everything going? I'm writing to invite you and Lisa to spend your summer holidays in Xinfeng for one week.

As far as I know, you are very interested in Chinese culture. It is a good chance for you to learn more about the local culture. I have made a schedule for you and I will take you to the most famous tourist attractions, such as Yunji Mountain, Yuntianhai Hot Spring, Yan Tower and so on. During this trip, you can not only see a lot of beautiful scenery but also taste delicious local food. In addition, Xiao Hong will book the flights and the hotel for you in advance.

I hope you can accept my invitation, and I am sure Xinfeng will leave a deep impression on you. Please let me know if you want to come before this Thursday. We long for your coming.

I am looking forward to your reply.

Yours,

Li Hua

Unit 2 The Source of Hakka Dialect

2.1 Listening: Different English Accents

2.2 Speaking: Different Hakka dialects

2.3 Reading 1

The Road to A Prosperous Dialect

In Guangdong, Guangxi, Fujian, Jiangxi, Hunan, Sichuan, Taiwan and other places across the sea, there lives an **active** community. They share particular customs and characteristics[①]. Although **settling down** in various areas, they are **recognized** to have the same **identity**—Hakka people, who **actually** speak the same language, Hakka dialect.

Hakka dialect, known as a tone language, is one of the seven **dialects** in China. **Going through** a long history of development, it is not **destroyed** but prospers[②]. It

① characteristic *n*. 特性。

② prosper *v*. 兴旺; 发达。

turns to be a dialect system which remains most archaisms[①]. What reliable research shows is that compared to the **official** language, Mandarin[②], Hakka dialect differs in three aspects.

First, it varies from Mandarin in phonetics[③]. In Hakka, a large amount of **vocabulary** starts with voiceless consonants[④] while in Mandarin it is expected to be voiced ones, such as the word "地" and "弟"[⑤]. Secondly, they are different in vocabulary. On the one hand, Hakka dialect remains a lot of words from archaisms such as using "面" to express "脸", "乌" to express "黑"; on the other hand, Hakka dialect is often prefixe[⑥] or suffixed[⑦] with some particular words, like "阿" and "佬"[⑧] to represent a close relationship or a job. **Finally**, they differ in tone, for Hakka dialect has a system of rich tones.

Though Hakka people come from different areas in the world, they basically have no difficulty in communicating with one another. And this well explains Hakka dialect's prosperity.

---

① archaism *n.*不再使用的古语。

② Mandarin *n.* 普通话。

③ phonetics *n.* 语音；语音学。

④ voiceless consonant 送气音。

⑤ "地" "弟"（客家话发［ti］，升调；普通话发［di］，去声）。

⑥ prefix *v.* 加前缀。

⑦ suffix *v.* 加后缀。

⑧ "阿" "佬"：人们称呼"爷爷"为"阿公"，"叔叔"为"阿叔"，普通话中却没有这一词头；客家话常在职业后加"佬"字，如剃头佬、打铁佬。

2.4 Reading 2

Ivy's puzzle[①]

Ivy, aged 43, is a foreign language teacher from Serbia[②], **Eastern** Europe. This July, she **finally** realized her long-lasting dream: stepping onto Chinese land, knowing about China and talking to Chinese people **face to face**. During the interview, she expressed her true thoughts about Xinfeng. She **added** that she was able to communicate with others in simple Chinese **at present**.

The long **journey** wore her out[③]. Luckily, it didn't discourage her fondness of China. After arriving here, she started to teach English at the Children's Palace. She recalled her first experience of having lunch in a local restaurant. Entering the restaurant, she ordered herself a local dish by using Mandarin with less fluency. While waiting for the meal, she noticed that when customers came in, the waiter would greet them by saying "Shi di mai?" And after they paid the money, the waiter usually responded with the word "wu guai". As a language teacher, she guessed it might be "Can I help you?" and "Thank you!" in English. But she kept wondering why it sounded so different from what she had learned from her Chinese teacher. Then, she **made up her mind** to **turn to** Linda, her boss for help.

As a **native**, Linda solved Ivy's puzzle. She explained patiently that people who live in Xinfeng tend to[④] speak dialect rather than Mandarin. Nowadays, all schools teach their courses in Mandarin. And the younger generations also **prefer** to speak this official language. However, getting used to the local dialect, the older generations turn

① puzzle *n*. 难题；难解之谜。

② Serbia 塞尔维亚。

③ wear sb. out 使某人疲惫。

④ tend to 倾向于。

to the opposite[①]. What Linda said greatly aroused[②] Ivy's interest, she was determined to explore more about the dialect.

2.5 Writing: A Letter of Suggestion

假设你是李华，新丰本地人。你读了《Ivy的困惑》这篇文章后，打算给Ivy一些关于学习客家话的建议。请你以建议信的形式，写一封信给Ivy, 内容包括你对客家话的看法，以及学习客家话的具体建议。要求观点明晰，语句连贯通顺，字数不少于150。

Dear Ivy,

____

I am looking forward to your reply.

Yours,

Li Hua

① opposite *adj.* 相反的。

② arouse *v.* 激起。

附翻译：

第二单元　客家话的来源

2.1 Listening：不同的英语口音（看视频）

2.2 Speaking：不同的客家方言（小话剧）

2.3 Reading 1

客家话的饶有兴味

在广东、广西、福建、江西、湖南、四川、台湾以及海外，居住着一个活跃的族群。他们有着共同的特性和风俗。虽然定居的地域不同，但他们有一个共同的身份——客家人。事实上，他们说着相同的语言——客家话。

客家话，是一种声调语言，属于汉语七大方言之一。经过漫长的发展历史，它不但没有被破坏，反而成为中华民族保留古语最多的一个方言体系。可靠的研究表明，它与官方语音——普通话相比，具有三大差异。

首先，语音的差异。客家话的语音中，很多在普通话中为浊音的词汇在客家话中都变成了送气音，如“地、弟”。其次，词汇的差异。一方面，客家方言对比于普通话，沿用古代词语较多，如称“脸”为“面”，称“黑”为“乌”。另一方面，客家话很多词语带有词头、词尾。常见的如“阿”（阿公、阿婆、阿叔等），“佬”（剃头佬、打铁佬、撑船佬）等。最后客家话与普通话存在声调的差异。

虽然客家人居住在世界各地，但基本上不存在沟通障碍。这也是客家话生命力的一种体现。

2.4 Reading 2

Ivy的困惑

Ivy,一名来自东欧塞尔维亚的外语教师，今年43岁。今年7月，她终于实现了她一直以来的梦想——踏上中国的土地，认识中国，面对面与中国的朋友交谈。在采访中，Ivy与我们表达了她对新丰的看法。她补充说，目前她已经能够使用简单的中文交际用语。

跋山涉水的旅行使Ivy很疲惫，幸运的是并没有消磨她对这片土地的喜爱。来到中国之后，Ivy开始了她在少年宫教英语的工作。她回忆第一次走进当地的一家餐厅，准备体验一番地道的中餐。她用不太流利的中文点了一份当地菜。但是在等待的过程中，她发现每个人进来的时候，老板都会问一句“食滴蛮来”，每个人付账之后，服务员都会点头说一句“不该不该”。作为一位语言教师，她猜测这两句话应该是英文的“Can I help you?”和“Thank you!”但是，她在心底默默好奇，为什么这听起来跟她的中文教师教的不一样。然后，她决定去向她的老板Linda问个究竟。

作为本地人，Linda解决了她的困惑。她耐心地解释道，住在新丰的人比起说普通话，更喜欢说方言。让今，所有学校里都进行普通话教学，年轻一辈更喜欢以普通话进行交流。然而，中老一辈则相反，更习惯用本土语言。Linda的回答激起了Ivy的好奇心，她决心对客家话进行更多的探究。

2.5 Writing：建议信

附参考范文：

Dear Ivy,

I'm glad to know that you have great interest in learning Hakka Dialect. Known as a tone language, Hakka dialect is recognized to be one of the seven dialects in China. It actually builds up a natural bridge to connect with those who speak the same language across the world. If you are determined to learn this kind of language, here are some suggestions to follow. To start with, it is useful for you to spend most of your spare time talking with the local people, which is surely the most effective way to learn a language. Then, if possible, you are advised to live with a local family. It gives you a better understanding and a huge passion for this language. What's more, you can try to keep a diary in Hakka dialect. And try to read it as often as you can in the morning. Hope you make great progress in learning this.

I'm looking forward to your reply.

Yours,

Li Hua

Unit 3 Xinfeng River

3.1 Listening and Speaking

Lugu River National Wetland Park

Watch the video once again and answer the following questions.

Located in the **southeast** of Xinfeng County, Lugu River National Wetland Park of Guangdong was built with the approval of National Forestry and Grassland Administration[①] in December 2014. To the rivers of the upper reaches of the Lugu River, the Lugu River Reservoir[②], the lower reaches of the Lugu River and their intersection[③] with the Xinfeng River as the main body, Lugu River National Wetland Park includes the dam on the Lugu River, the river stream and the surrounding water source conservation[④] forest of 50 to 300 meters, flowing from south-north. The total planned area of the park is 469.54 hectares[⑤], and the total wetland area is 153.46 hectares. The wetland rate is 32.68%. Mainly consisting of artificial reservoirs, natural

① National Forestry and Grassland Administration 国家林业和草原局。

② reservoir *n.* 水库。

③ intersection *n.* 交叉点。

④ conservation *n.* 保护；保存。

⑤ hectare *n.* 公顷。

rivers and secondary forests around lakes, the wetland-forest composite[①] wetland ecosystem is typical in the subtropical[②] mountain regions of China.

The Wetland Park belongs to the Dongjiang river system. Its main waters are Lugu River and Lugu River Reservoir. Lugu River is the secondary tributary[③] of Dongjiang River and the primary tributary of the Xinfeng River Reservoir（Wanlv Lake）which is the largest reservoir in Guangdong. The park is located on the northern edge of the Tropic of Cancer[④]. The terrain[⑤] is high in the north and low in the south. With undulating[⑥] mountains, vertical and horizontal[⑦] streams and dense forests, it has **a great number of** climate characteristics[⑧], such as plentiful rainfall, distinct seasons, and short winter but long summer. There are abundant[⑨] species of wild animals and plants in the park, including 1,208 species of vascular plants[⑩] and 438 species of wild vertebrates[⑪], 40 species are listed under state key protection, which has important protection value in terms of biodiversity[⑫].

（1）When was Xinfeng Lugu River National Wetland Park of Guangdong built?

（2）How many species are there in the park in total?

附答案：

（1）It was built in December 2014.

---

① composite *adj.* 复合的。

② subtropical *adj.* 亚热带的。

③ secondary tributary *n.* 二级支流。

④ the Tropic of Cancer 北回归线。

⑤ terrain *n.* 地势。

⑥ undulating *adj.* 波浪起伏的。

⑦ vertical and horizontal *adj.* 垂直的和水平的。

⑧ characteristic *n.* 特征。

⑨ abundant *adj.* 丰富的。

⑩ vascular plant 维管植物。

⑪ vertebrate *n.* 脊椎动物。

⑫ biodiversity *n.* 生物多样性。

(2) There are a total of 1646 species in the park.

3.2 Reading 1

Xinfeng River

Dear **judges** and fellows,

It is my great honor to introduce the mother river of our hometown, Xingfeng River which has a long history.

First of all, I would like to ask you a question. Do you **prefer** to live in a quiet suburb? If so, then Xinfeng is the place for you. Many people in the surrounding cities **are fond of** travelling to Xinfeng. Moreover, **because of** its promising development, many college **graduates** have **determined** to return here for development.

As we all know, Xingfeng River is named after Xinfeng County. It is a tributary of the Dongjiang River of the Pearl River system. With a total length of 163 kilometers, it originates[①] from Yunji Mountain in Xinfeng, and its catchment area[②] is 5,813 square kilometers. A hydropower station[③] has been **set up** in the lower reaches of Xinfeng River, only 6 kilometers away from Heyuan City, forming Xingfeng River Reservoir (also known as Wanlv Lake), one of the largest artificial[④] lakes in Guangdong province. The high-**quality** water of Xingfeng River not only feeds Xinfeng people, but also directly benefits thousands of people in Guangzhou, Shenzhen, Hong Kong and so on. The Xingfeng River is **so important that** Xinfeng residents[⑤] **take good care of** it, because many people will be affected once it is polluted.

---

① originate *v.* 起源。

② catchment area 集水面积。

③ hydropower station 水电站。

④ artificial *adj.* 人工的。

⑤ resident *n.* 居民。

Xingfeng River is a symbol of Xinfeng. As a Xinfeng **native**, I believe that it is everyone's responsibility to protect Xinfeng River and **make good use of** every drop of water. Hereby, I **sincerely** invite all of you to visit Xinfeng and appreciate the beauty of Xinfeng River. Thank you for your listening.

3.3 Reading 2

Journey to Yunji Mountain

Sunday 11th November, 2018

Although I have been to Yunji Mountain many times **ever since** I was born, this trip was totally a different one, so I must **set it down**.

It was our head teacher Chen **who** organized us to climb Yunji Mountain and take pictures for the competition. At the beginning, we all **made up our minds** to take part in it, but several classmates **changed their minds** the day before **because of** personal matters. However, Teacher Chen **persuaded** them to go together. **As usual**, our **reliable** monitor Carol was responsible for setting the **schedule**, arranging **transportation** and preparing prizes.

After **packing up** some necessities[①], we took the bus from the school gate at 5:30 in the morning. At the foot of Yunji Mountain, the air was **so fresh that** we came to life **right away**. While climbing, we helped each other. **Even if** there were all kinds of difficulties, no one **gave in**. **Finally**, all of us successfully climbed to the top.

Tired as we were, we **had fun singing and laughing** along the way. When the charming scenery **came into our view, we could hardly wait** to take photos from every angle[②]. In the end, Peter won the competition for taking many photos of our classmates' laughing faces, but he insisted that he should share his prize with

① necessity *n.* 必需品。

② angle *n.* 角度。

everyone.

In my opinion, it was our mutual[1] help that made this activity more meaningful and unforgettable. I am looking forward to our next team-building activity.

3.4 Writing: Speech

假设你是李华。你将参加一次英语演讲比赛（Speech Contest），主题是向外地人介绍秀田古树公园。请参照以下要点写一份演讲稿。

要点如下：

1. 秀田古树公园位于新丰县马头镇，离县城十多千米。

2. 两棵四百多年历史的古秋枫树（Autumn maple）是那里的主要景点（Attraction）。古树保护区还包括绿地、园林（Garden）、秋水湖等景观。

3. 邀请大家过来游玩，感受新丰文化。

注意：

1. 词数100左右。

2. 可以适当增加细节，使行文连贯。

Dear judges and fellows,

____

____

____

____

____

____

I am looking forward to your reply.

Yours,

Li Hua

① mutual *adj.* 相互的。

附翻译：

第三单元　新丰江

3.1 Listening and Speaking

鲁古河国家湿地公园

再看一遍录像并回答问题。

广东新丰鲁古河国家湿地公园于2014年12月经国家林业和草原局批准建设，地处新丰县的东南部，以鲁古河上游河流山背塅、鲁古河水库、鲁古河下游至与新丰江交汇处为主体，包括鲁古河上的水坝、入河溪流以及周边50～300米的水源涵养林，呈南北走向。公园规划总面积为469.54公顷，湿地总面积为153.46公顷，湿地率为32.68%，以人工水库、自然河流、环湖次生林等组成的森林复合湿地生态系统是我国亚热带山地区的典型特征。

鲁古河国家湿地公园属东江水系，主要水域为鲁古河和鲁古河水库，是广东最大的水库——新丰江水库（万绿湖）的一级支流，是东江的二级支流。公园地处北回归线北缘，境内地势北高南低，山峦起伏，溪流纵横，森林茂密，具有雨量充沛、四季分明、夏长冬短等丰富的气候特征。公园内野生动植物物种丰富，有维管植物1208种，野生脊椎动物438种，列入国家重点保护的动植物有40种之多，在生物多样性方面具有重要的保护价值。

（1）广东新丰鲁古河国家湿地公园建于什么时候?

（2）公园内一共有多少种动植物?

附答案：

（1）它建于2014年12月。

（2）公园内一共有1646种动植物。

3.2 Reading 1

新丰江

敬爱的评委老师们和同学们：

很荣幸能为大家介绍我家乡源远流长的母亲江——新丰江。

首先，我想问大家一个问题。你是否更喜欢住在安静的郊区？如果是的话，那么新丰正是适合你的地方。很多周边城市的人喜欢到新丰旅游。而且，因为新丰很有发展前景，很多大学毕业生也决定回到家乡就业。

众所周知，新丰江因新丰县而得名。它是珠江水系东江的一条支流，发源于新丰县的云髻山，全长163千米，集水面积为5813平方千米。在距河源市仅6千米的新丰江下游建立了一个水电站，形成了广东省最大的人工湖——新丰江水库（又称万绿湖）。新丰江的优质水不仅造福新丰人，还直接惠泽广州、深圳、香港等千万民众。新丰江如此重要，以至于新丰人民悉心爱护着它,因为一旦它被污染，很多人将受到影响。

新丰江是新丰的象征之一。作为一个新丰本地人，我认为保护并利用好新丰江的每一滴水是每个人的责任。在此，我也诚邀大家来新丰旅游，一睹新丰江的风采。谢谢。

3.3 Reading 2

云髻山游记

2018年11月11日，星期天

虽然自我出生以来已经去过云髻山很多次了，但这次是截然不同的一次经历，所以我必须将其记录下来。

正是我们班主任陈老师组织我们一起去爬云髻山并拍照进行比赛的。一开始，大家都决定参加，但有几个同学前一天因为私事改变主意。然而，陈老师说服他们一起去。如平常一样，我们可靠的班长Carol负责安排日程，安排交通和准备奖品。

当天，我们在打包了一些必需品后，我们早晨五点半坐公共汽车从校门口出发。到了云髻山脚下，那里的空气如此清新，以至于我们立刻清醒。在爬山的过程中，我们相互帮助。即使过程中有各种各样的困难，但是没有一个人放弃。最终，我们所有人都成功登顶。

虽然我们很累，但是我们一路有说有笑，很开心。当那迷人的景色进入视野时，我们都迫不及待地从各种角度拍照。最后，Peter因为拍了很多同学的笑脸而赢得比赛，但他坚持要把奖品分享给大家。

在我看来，正是我们的相互帮助使得此次活动变得更有意义和令人难忘。我十分期待我们的下一次团队建设活动。

3.4 Writing：演讲

附参考范文：

Dear judges and fellows,

It is my great honor to introduce you to Xiutian Ancient Tree Park in our hometown.

The Xiutian Ancient Tree Park is located in Matou Town, Xinfeng County, more than 10 kilometers away from the main street of Matou. The main attractions there are two ancient autumn maple trees which have a history of more than 400 years. There are all kinds of views for you to enjoy, including grass, gardens, lakes and so on. Besides, you can taste some delicious local food there.

I sincerely invite all of you to travel here to enjoy the beautiful views here and know more about the local culture of Xinfeng.

I am looking forward to your reply.

Yours,

Li Hua

Unit 4　Cultural Relics in Xinfeng

4.1 Listening and Reading Aloud: Jiudongshibajing

"Jiudongshibajing" located in the Tanshi Village in Xinfeng County, was built in 1660 and finished 80 years later. There are three buildings on the cross[①] and three on the vertical[②], which makes it get the name "Jiudong", meaning nine buildings. And there are six dooryards[③] in each building. That's why there are "shibajing", which means 18 dooryards. Many valuable measures and materials were reserved here. Unfortunately, most of them got **in ruins**. Since the **foundation** of the People's Republic of China, these buildings have cultivated more than twenty people to study in colleges. **Ever since the** 1980s, people living there have moved out one after another. "Nowadays, 'Zhuwutang' is the name of the main hall[④]", said Wen Fuqiu, one of the villagers, "It means that we hope our families to become as flourishing[⑤] as banboos and as many talents as the phoenixes[⑥] in the sycamore tree[⑦]."

---

① cross *n*. 横向。

② vertical *n*. 纵向。

③ dooryard *n*. 天井。

④ main hall 大厅。

⑤ flourishing *adj*. 繁荣。

⑥ phoenix *n*. 凤凰。

⑦ sycamore tree 梧桐树。

4.2 Reading 1

Zhangtian Mooncake Mould and Dandingjiu

Xinfeng is a county with a long history and a large number of intangible cultural heritage[1]. The following material is the interview between Li Hua, a member of school journalist clubs, and Mr. Pan, the general director[2] of the Bureau of Culture[3] in Xinfeng. It is about Zhangtian Mooncake Mould[4] and "Dandingjiu".

Li Hua: Good morning. Can you introduce Zhangtian Mooncake Mould briefly to us?

Mr. Pan: Sure. Zhangtian Mooncake Mould, as is shown by the name, is the tool to make mooncakes. It is a traditional art of Zhangtian Village in Meikeng Town, which was invented by the ancestors[5] of the Zhangs' family.

Li Hua: Then how is a Zhangtian Mooncake Mould made?

Mr. Pan: The making procedure[6] includes painting, engraving[7] and other complicated[8] techniques. The engraver will draw some characters, animals and flowers **in order to** show the values of laboring people[9] in expecting safety, reunion[10] and affluence[11].

Li Hua: That is to say, it is very helpful to the strengthen Chinese sense of self-identity[12] in traditional culture and sense of belonging!

---

① intangible cultural heritage 非物质文化遗产。

② the general director 局长。

③ Bureau of Culture 文化局。

④ Zhangtian Mooncake Mould 张田饼印。

⑤ ancestor *n.* 祖先。

⑥ procedure *n.* 流程。

⑦ engrave *v.* 雕刻。

⑧ complicated *adj.* 复杂的。

⑨ laboring people 劳动人民。

⑩ reunion *n.* 团圆。

⑪ affluence *n.* 富足。

⑫ sense of self-identity 自我认同感。

Mr. Pan: Exactly right. However, fewer and fewer people **are willing to** engage in the making of Zhangtian Mooncake Mould. **Because of** that, the government has taken measures to protect this skill. **In addition to** this, there is another famous heritage called Dandingjiu.

Li Hua: Dandingjiu? Is it a kind of wine that we can drink?

Mr. Pan: Not **exactly**. It is the name of a traditional folk activity held by Lais' family① in Yaotian Town, which was originally used to encourage their families to give birth to boy babies **in order to** make their family more prosperous② and protect themselves from being bullied③ by other families. There are four stages: sacrificing④ ancestors, **setting off** the firecrackers, rushing for the offerings⑤, and lion dancing, among which rushing for the offerings is the most lively part. The family **holding** this activity will move the offerings out to the square⑥, and all people **present**, whether they are his family or not, will be allowed to rush for food. The more quickly the offerings are gone, the happier the host family will become, because it indicates⑦ that the host family will get more and more prosperous.

Li Hua: How interesting!

Mr. Pan: Till now, every family will hold Dandingjiu even after they give birth to a girl baby.

4.3 Reading 2

The Depressed Xinfeng "Dema"

After interviewing Mr. Pan, Li Hua went to Yaotian downtown to **look for** more

① Lais' family 赖氏家族。

② prosperous *adj*. 繁荣的。

③ bully *v*. 欺负。

④ sacrifice *v*. 祭奠。

⑤ offerings *n*. 祭品。

⑥ square *n*. 广场。

⑦ indicate *v*. 预示。

heritage there. **All of a sudden**, he heard an old lady yelling, "Excellent 'Dema', Excellent 'Dema'..." Then another interesting interview cane.

Li Hua: Good afternoon. What is "Dema"?

The old lady: As you can see, this kind of hat is called "Dema". It is a tool that people **used to get rid of** sunshine and rain. In the past, every of the older generation① here was able to make "Dema" **by themselves**.

Li Hua: How much is it?

The old lady: 25 *yuan* for each.

Li Hua: Oh, a bit expensive.

The old lady:It is worth that price. It is very complicated to make a "Dema". The bamboos used should be **more than** three years old. Then **cut out** the two ends② of the bamboos to get the middle parts and cut them into thin peels and weave③. After **covering** them **with** some soft bamboo leaves and cement paper④, people need to wipe on the tung oil or pine sesame oil and dry them to make it a "Dema".

Li Hua: Yes, what a complicated process. Does it sell well?

The old lady: When I was young, we wove "Dema" to **make a living** for our families. Although it was cheap, it sold well and we could earn much from it. Later, every family became richer and richer, which makes it possible to buy some umbrellas and raincoats. That is to say, "Dema" is gradually out of people's choices.

Li Hua: What a pity! Such a wonderful craft! I would like to buy one.

4.4 Writing: Make a poster

Make a poster to introduce the specialties of your living town.

---

① older generation 老一代。

② end *n.* 末端。

③ weave *v.* 编织。

④ cement paper 水泥纸。

附翻译：

第四单元 新丰文化遗产

4.1 Listening and Reading Aloud：九栋十八井

“九栋十八井”位于新丰县潭石村，始建于1660年，历时80多年竣工。建成横三栋、纵三栋，名谓九栋；每栋各有六口天井，共为十八井，故称九栋十八井。九栋十八井一直保存有许多宝贵的文物资料，可惜后来被损毁。从中华人民共和国成立至今，该围屋共培育出二十多名大学生。自20世纪80年代初起，居住在九栋十八井里的人们陆陆续续地往外搬。“现在，竹梧堂仍然是我们温氏家族的堂号。”温福球说道，“也寄托着我们希望家族像竹子成林、雨后春笋一样生生不息，像梧桐树一样筑巢引凤、人才辈出。”

4.2 Reading 1

张田饼印、担丁酒

新丰县历史悠久，非物质文化遗产众多。下面是我校记者团成员李华对我县文化局局长潘先生进行的关于张田饼印、担丁酒的采访实录。

李华：您好！您能简要介绍一下张田饼印吗？

潘先生：好的。张田饼印是制作月饼的工具。张田饼印是梅坑镇张田村的传统艺术，由张田村张姓祖先所创。

李华：张田饼印是如何制作的呢？

潘先生：张田饼印制作过程包含美术、雕刻等比较复杂的技术，有人物、动物和花卉等图案，体现了劳动人民祈求吉祥、团圆、富足的价值观。

李华：这样说，张田饼印很有利于增进中华民族传统文化认同感和归属感啊。

潘先生：确实是，但是愿意从事饼印雕刻的人越来越少，因此，当地政府已经采取措施来保护这项技能。除了张田饼印，我们县的担丁酒也很出名。

李华：担丁酒？这是一种喝的酒吗？

潘先生：不全是，这其实是我们县遥田镇赖姓族人的一项传统民俗活动，其初衷是鼓励本姓族人多生男丁以兴旺家族，增强凝聚力，以免受外姓人的欺负。“担丁酒”分四个阶段：“祭祖公”“鸣炮”“抢丁酒”“瑞狮庆贺”，“抢丁酒”是活动的高潮。办担丁酒的人家把祭祖的食品搬到祠外广场摆好，所有在场的男性老少（小孩居多）去争抢祭过祖先的食品，谁家的担丁酒被抢得越快，家族 就会变得越幸福，以示本家族人丁越兴旺。

李华：太有趣了！

潘先生：发展至今，生了女孩的家庭也会办担丁酒。

4.3 Reading 2

失落的新丰“得麻”

采访完潘先生，李华去到了遥田镇街，想寻找更多关于遥田的文化遗产，突然听到街边老奶奶的吆喝声，“卖‘得麻’了，卖‘得麻’了……”一段有趣的采访由此展开。

李华：下午好，“得麻”是什么？

老奶奶：“得麻”就是这种帽子，是人们曾经常备的遮阳挡雨工具。过去，我们这里的老一辈家家户户都会自己织“得麻”。

李华：“得麻”多少钱一顶啊？

老奶奶：25元一顶。

李华：哦，有一点贵。

老奶奶：它值得这个价。“得麻”的制作过程很复杂，用的竹子要长超过三年，然后裁去两头竹节，留取中间的部分切成小叶片来编织。然后覆盖一层泡软的大竹叶和一层水泥纸，最后还要擦上桐油、松香油晾干，才完成所有的工序。

李华：多么复杂的过程啊。“得麻”卖得好吗？

老奶奶：小时候，我们家靠织“得麻”来谋生，虽然收入微薄，但比较畅销，我们可以从中赚很多的钱。到后来，家家户户经济条件都好了，大家都买雨伞雨衣了，“得麻”就不好卖了。

李华：太可惜了，这么好的工艺。那我买一顶吧。

4.4 Writing：做海报

做一张海报，介绍你所在镇区的特产。

附海报评价标准：

学生所在镇区特产海报评价标准	
1	结构齐全，应包含海报题目，适当粘贴镇区特产的图片或自行绘画，辅以简洁的英文说明
2	倡导学生使用列要点式创作或使用小标题式创作
3	上交的海报可在全班范围内进行优秀海报评选

Unit 5 Xinfeng Celebrities

5.1 Listening and Speaking: Introduction to Zheng Xuanmin

Watch a video and design three questions according to the content.

Zheng Xuanmin was born into a poor rural family in 1916. As his family couldn't support his education, the government and his relatives offered to help him continue his studies. He graduated from primary school in 1933. During his teenage period, Japanese invaders invaded China, which made the Chinese nation caught in a miserable time. In April 1939, he joined the Communist Party of China and taught as a teacher to carry out his work in the Party. He was enthusiastic in advertising for the Communist party of China by putting up some posters, having some performances and so on. In February 1941, when some people felt depressed, he encouraged people in time. He said: "Only by striving can we raise the sun in our mind." He also united the teenagers by teaching them songs like *Huanghe chorus*. He taught in many places and at last he was asked to organize the anti-Japanese troops in Huilong. Unfortunately, he was caught by enemies and killed on the way to the center of Shaoguan City. At that time, he was only 29 years old.

After the People's Republic of China was built, in memory of Zheng Xuanmin, Xinfeng No. 1 Middle School was named after him as "Xuanmin Middle School".

5.2 Reading 1

The Revolutionary Martyr[①]——Li Renyu

In 1903, a boy was born into a poor peasant's[②] family in Fengcheng Town in Xinfeng. His mother died when he was a little kid. He **had got to** spend his childhood mainly in his grandfather's house, the Pan's Family Compound[③]. Supported by his uncle, he was sent to Shaoguan and Guangzhou for study. Influenced by the thoughts about revolutionary, he **joined** the Communist Party[④] of China.

He took part in the famous event named Guangzhou Uprising[⑤] in December, 1927. Later, with the **guidance** of the major comrades[⑥] from the Fourth Red Army, he led an army to tightly unite the populace[⑦] to support the revolution. The Western Fujian Revolutionary **base** was finally built up, and people strongly believed it would be hard to achieve without their efforts. At that time, his name was just put after Mao Zedong, Zhu De and Chen Yi on the committee[⑧] member list of the Fourth Red Army. On September 30th, 1932, he went to Baoding, hoping to secretly transfer a mimeograph[⑨] and other things. However, he was betrayed and captured. He **suffered** from all kinds of torture in jail, but he never **gave in**. He **made up his mind** to **devote**

---

① revolutionary martyr 革命烈士。

② peasant *n*. ［从前的或贫穷国家的］农民；佃农。

③ the Pan's Family Compound 潘氏故居大院。

④ Communist Party 共产党。

⑤ Guangzhou Uprising 广州起义。

⑥ comrade *n*. 同志。

⑦ populace *n*. 百姓；大众。

⑧ committee *n*. 委员会。

⑨ mimeograph *n*. 油印机。

himself to the revolution. On November 27th in the same year, he sacrificed his life for liberation.

In May, 2000, Li Renyu was **recognized** as a revolutionary martyr by the People's Government of Guangdong Province. And almost two years later, a statue was **set up** to remember him and his **selfless quality** in Nanmentang Square in Xinfeng, and in the meantime, the square was named after him.

5.3 Reading 2

Adam's story

My name is Adam. I **grew up** in a big family in Xinfeng. My father is the eldest child. Among my uncles and aunts, the most impressed is the fourth one, Uncle Paul. Uncle Paul was a village cadre① in our hometown and always tried his best to **help** the villagers **out**. He was meditative② and seldom laughed in public, and I rarely talked to such a serious man like him. **Every time when** the Spring Festival came, he would cook silently in the kitchen to prepare a feast③ for us. On the eve of last Spring Festival, I **was looking forward to** having another delicious feast. I bought some beef and pork and drove toward our village. However, I would never have a chance to taste the familiar reunion dinner.

It was abnormally④ hot and dry that day. The minute I arrived at the entrance of the village, I was dragged by Uncle Huang to the edge of a mountain. Uncle Huang said nothing all the way until I saw a burned body on the ground, beyond

① village cadre 村干部。

② meditative *adj.* 少言的。

③ feast *n.* 盛宴。

④ abnormally *adv.* 异常地。

recognition. Even before Uncle Huang hadn't told me the truth, I realized it was my Uncle Paul.

According to Uncle Huang, I **got to know** the whole process of the accident. On that afternoon, a village **turned to** them for help to deal with the mountain fire. They three' including Uncle Paul' rushed to the scene to rescue. Uncle Paul always considered the village as his own home. He rushed at the very front of them and got farther and farther. They **were about** to put out the fire **when** a strong wind blew and the fire **came to life** again and swallowed my Uncle Paul. Although having gotten burnt by the fire, Uncle Huang and another cadre rushed into the fire sea to rescue Uncle Paul without hesitation. They managed to move Uncle Paul to a safe place, however, he never **came to himself** again. **Finally**, the firemen arrived and **thanks to** the three cadres' efforts, the firemen put out the fire quickly and made the whole village peaceful again. The arsonist <u>was sentenced to</u>① three years for setting fire **on purpose**.

However, my Uncle Paul would stay to guard the forest forever, and **devote** all his life **to** the village **as well**.

5.4 Writing: A Letter of Gratitude

假如你是李华，是学校的篮球队队长，篮球明星Grady上学期资助了你所在的篮球队，请你代表学校篮球队，写信给Grady表示感谢。请包括以下要点：

1. 感谢Grady无私地资助篮球队贫困学生，让他们可以安心学习。

2. 简要介绍一下校篮球队队员在受资助后的变化。

① be sentenced to 被判刑。

注意：

1. 词数不少于100，开头和结尾已经给出，不计入总词数。

2. 不得使用真实姓名和学校名称。

3. 适当补充细节。

Dear Grady,

I am writing to offer our thanks to you for your funding. ________________

____

____

____

____

____

____

____

____

____

____

____

____

____

____

I am looking forward to your reply.

Yours,

Li Hua

附翻译：

第五单元　新丰名人

5.1 Listening and Speaking：介绍郑选民

看一段视频，根据视频内容设计三个问题并回答。

1916年，郑选民出生在一个贫穷的农村家庭。因为他家境贫寒无法支撑他的学业，政府和亲戚主动帮他继续了学业。1933年，郑选民小学毕业。在他的青少年时代，日本人侵略中国，导致中华民族遭受了深重的苦难。1939年4月，他加入中国共产党，并以教师职业为掩护，开展党的工作。他通过张贴海报、进行表演等一系列方式富有热情地宣传中国共产党。1941年2月，当部分人感到沮丧的时候，他及时地鼓舞了大家。他说："只有通过奋斗，我们才能在心中升起一轮太阳。"他还通过教青年人唱《黄河大合唱》这样的歌来团结他们。他在很多地方讲过学，最后他被任命在回龙负责组建抗日部队。不幸的是，他后来落入敌手，并被押往韶关杀害，时年29岁。

中华人民共和国成立后，县委、县人民政府将新丰一中改名为"选民中学"，以示对他的纪念。

5.2 Reading 1

革命烈士——李任予

1903年，李任予出生于丰城镇一个贫农家庭，年少失母。孩提时代他不得不居住在外公家的潘氏故居大院。受舅父资助，李任予先后于韶关和广州求学，受到革命的熏陶，加入中国共产党。

1927年12月参加了著名的"广州起义"。后来，在红四军的领导指挥下，他率领部队发动群众，为闽西革命根据地的建立做出了贡献。当时在红四军委员会委员名单中，他被排在毛泽东、朱德、陈毅之后。1932年9月30日，李任予按约定时间到保定与一位同志商议转移油印机等物时，被出卖逮捕。其间遭受各种酷刑，但他没有屈服。他决心献身于革命。1932年11月27日，李任予为了解放事业献出了宝贵的生命。

2000年5月，经广东省人民政府批准，追认李任予为革命烈士。将近两年后，新丰县委、县政府为了纪念李任予和他无私的品质，在新丰县南门塘文化广场竖起李任予烈士铜像，并将该广场命名为“任予广场”。

5.3 Reading 2

亚当的故事

我是亚当，成长在新丰的一个大家庭。父亲是家中的老大，在父亲的兄弟姐妹中，我印象最深刻的是我的四叔。他是一名村干部，兢兢业业，经常为村民提供力所能及的帮助。他少言而很少在公开场合笑，我也甚少和他交流。逢年过节时，他总是默默地在厨房给我们做好吃的。去年除夕前一天，我期待着能吃上四叔做的年夜饭，还兴致勃勃地买了猪肉和牛肉，开车前往老家。但是，我再也吃不到往昔的味道了。

那天天气异常燥热。我刚到村口，就被村委的黄叔拉到山边。黄叔什么也没 说，直到我看到地上有一具无法辨认烧焦的尸体。在黄叔告诉我之前，我就意识到那是四叔。

据黄叔回忆，那天下午突然有村民向他们求助，说村口的山边着火了。他们三名村干部包括四叔马上赶往现场救火。四叔一向视村为家，冲在了最前头，慢慢与队友拉开了距离。当胜利在望时，一阵风吹来，回火了，火无情地吞噬着这位守护村园的干部。虽已被灼伤，黄叔他们还是毫不犹豫地救出了四叔。他们设法把四叔带动一个安全的地方，但是他再也没有苏醒过来。最后，消防员终于来了，在四叔他们灭火的基础上，快速地灭了火，还给了村庄安宁。纵火者因为故意纵火被判刑三年。

然而，我的四叔永远守护在这一片山林，并把他的一生都奉献给了这个村庄了。

5.4 Writing：感谢信

附参考范文：

Dear Grady,

I am writing to offer our thanks to you for your funding.

You are our idol. We appreciate you so much that we feel powerful with your kindness. It is selfless of you to raise money for poor students in our basketball team. Thanks for your help, they can play basketball and study without any trouble. At present, they have made some progress in their study. What's more, they give a hand to others in daily life. Thank you again and best wishes.

I am looking forward to your reply.

Yours,

Li Hua

Exercise

Unit 1 Brief Introduction to Xinfeng

Reading 1

1. Comprehension

Read the passage carefully and choose the correct answers to the following questions.

(1) Why did the author and her husband go on a trip to Xinfeng?

A. Xinfeng is not far from Guangzhou.

B. There are a lot of amazing scenes in Xinfeng.

C. They didn't know how to spend their national holiday.

D. They wanted to relax themselves from the stressful work.

(2) Which of the following statements is not correct?

A. The author has not been to Xinfeng before.

B. The author didn't notice the scenery along the way.

C. The author thought Xinfeng is not far from Guangzhou.

D. The author and her husband will spend their entire National holiday in Xinfeng.

(3) What's the author's attitude to Xinfeng?

A. Depressed.

B. Concerned.

C. Negative.

D. Positive.

2. Learning about Language

Please use the given words, phrases or sentence patterns to translate the following sentences.

(1) 这是我第三次遇到他了。(It is/was the + 序数词 +time that...)

(2) 当爬上云髻山山顶的时候，我们都没有丧失勇气。(While doing..., lose heart)

(3) 你一到达新丰，就会爱上这里迷人的风景。(fall in love)

(4) 正如你所知，我以身为一名新丰人而自豪。(as you know, be proud of/that...)

(5) 事实上，过去十年见证(witness)了新丰快速的发展。(as a matter of fact)

Reading 2

1. Comprehension

Read the diary carefully and fill in the table about the introduction of the Yan Tower.

Location		
Time of building		
Who proposed it		
Appearance	inside	
	outside	
Why does it have reference value		

2. Learning about Language

Complete the passage with proper words or the proper forms of the given words.

Nowadays, more and more people prefer to join in （1）________（outdoors）activities in their spare time, especially travelling, so does my cousin Li Hua. However, he always （2）________（choose）to travel alone, which makes his mom （3）________（extreme）worried about his safety. Every time he has time for travelling, he is looking forward to （4）________（make）the trip by himself. Not surprisingly, he often gets （5）________（injure）or gets lost during the journey, because he keeps （6）________（ignore）others' suggestions that he should pay more attention to his own safety and be better prepared. Nevertheless, we can tell from his happy facial （7）________（express）that he always has （8）________ wonderful journey. He told us last time that although he travelled alone, he frequently met nice guys （9）________ were willing to help him on the way. No matter who helped him, he would express his gratitude to them （10）________（sincere）.

附参考答案：

Unit 1　Brief Introduction to Xinfeng

Reading 1

1.Comprehension

（1）D

（2）B

（3）D

2. Learning about Language

（1）It was the third time that I had met him.

（2）While climbing to the top of Yunji Mountain, none of us lost heart.

(3) Once you arrive in Xinfeng, you will fall in love with the charming scenery here.

(4) As you know, I am proud of being a native in Xinfeng.

(5) As a matter of fact, the last ten years have witnessed the rapid development of Xinfeng.

Reading 2

1. Comprehension

Location	on the top of the Laowei Mountain	
Time of building	1739	
Who proposed it	Chen Zhangyi	
Appearance	inside	13 wooden floors leading direct to the top floor
	outside	Made of seven floors
Why it has reference value	because of its unique structure and ancient style	

2. Learning about Language

(1) outdoor

(2) chooses

(3) extremely

(4) making

(5) injured

(6) ignoring

(7) expression

(8) a

(9) who

(10) sincerely

Unit 2 The Source of Hakka Dialect

Reading 1

1. Match the new words and expressions with their meanings

(1) recognize	A. the characteristics or beliefs that distinguish people from others
(2) identity	B. used in speaking to emphasize a fact or a comment
(3) actually	C. to know who sb. is or what sth. is when you see or hear them
(4) dialect	D. that can be trusted to do sth well
(5) reliable	E. The form of a language that is spoken in one area
(6) official	F. after a long time, especially when there has been some difficulty
(7) vocabulary	G. agreed to, said or done by sb. who is in a position of authority
(8) finally	H. all the words that a person knows or uses

2. Read the passage carefully and answer the following questions

(1) What does "an active community" in the first paragraph refer to?

(2) How many aspects is Hakka dialect different from China's official language, Mandarin? And which aspect impresses you most?

(3) What do you think of the suffix "佬" in today's society? Will you support for such a suffix?

Reading 2

1. Read the passage and put these sentences in the right sequence

A. She started to teach English at the Children's Palace.

B. The long journey wore her out.

C. As a native, Linda solved Ivy's puzzle.

D. Then, she made up her mind to turn to Linda, her boss, for help.

E. She recalled her first experience of having lunch in a local restaurant.

2. Answer the following questions after reading the passage again

(1) What is Ivy's long-lasting dream?

(2) Did Ivy feel upset after such a long journey to arrive in China? And did this long journey discourage her fondness of China?

(3) Why did Ivy feel puzzled after she noticed the conversation between the waiter and the customer?

(4) Why do you think the older generation prefers to speak the local dialect?

附参考答案：

Unit 2 The Source of Hakka Dialect

Reading 1

1. Match the new words and expressions with their meanings

(1) C

(2) A

(3) B

(4) E

(5) D

(6) G

（7）H

（8）F

2. Read the passage carefully and answer the following questions

（1）It refers to Hakka people.

（2）Hakka dialects is different from Mandarin in three/ 3 aspects. And the second aspect impresses me most.

（3）In today's society, I think it sounds a bit rude or impolite for people to use such a suffix, which may be different from its original meaning in Hakka dialect. So I won't support it.

Reading 2

1. Read the passage and put these sentences in the right sequence

BAEDC

2. Answer the following questions after reading the passage again

（1）Her long-lasting dream is stepping onto Chinese land, knowing about China and talking to Chinese people face to face.

（2）Yes, she did feel upset. But the long journey did not discourage her fondness of China.

（3）Because what she heard in the restaurant sounded so different from what she had learned from her Chinese teacher.

（4）Maybe the older generation thinks Hakka dialect represents part of the tradition and they want to keep it.

Unit 3 Xingfeng River

Reading 1

1. Comprehension

Read the passage carefully and choose the correct answers to the following questions.

(1) What does the underline word "promising" mean in paragraph 2?

A. long and terrible

B. possible and excellent

C. unlikely but wonderful

D. continuous and disappointing

(2) Which of the following statements is correct according to the passage?

A. Xinfeng River has been polluted by the natives.

B. There is a hydropower station in Xinfeng County.

C. The water of Xinfeng River only benefits the natives.

D. People from all over the country like travelling to Xinfeng.

(3) What's the author's purpose in giving this speech?

A. To introduce Xinfeng.

B. To praise Xinfeng Natives.

C. To attract tourists and call for protection.

D. To tell people the importance of water.

2. Learning about Language

Complete the following sentences with the proper forms of the given words.

(1) Thanks to the local guide's ________ (introduce), I learned so much about the famous scenic spot.

(2) When I was a child, I ________ (prefer) playing outside to staying at home.

(3) After ________ (graduate) from the university, Tom started to work in Microsoft Company.

(4) We were surprised by his ________ (determine) that he would travel abroad alone.

(5) ________ (judge) from his sad look, we knew that he had a terrible day.

Reading 2

1. Comprehension

Read the passage carefully and write down what the following people's identity are and what they did in the activity.

Persons	Identity	What they did
Miss Chen		
Carol		
Peter		
All students	/	

2. Read the passage and answer thc following question

What did the author think of this activity? Why did the author think so?

3. Learning about Language

Please use the given words, phrases or sentence patterns to translate the following sentences.

(1) 正是Tom邀请我们去参加这次旅行的。(It is/was...that/who...强调句式)

(2) 即使没人相信你能做到，你也应该对自己有信心。(Even if...)

(3) 我妈妈坚持要求我一到广州就得打电话给她。(insist that...)

（4）一旦Tom下定决心，除了他自己，没有人能改变他的主意。（make up one's mind, change one's mind）

（5）我相信你会在派对上与朋友们开心地聊天的。（have fun doing sth.）

附参考答案：

Unit 3 Xingfeng River

Reading 1

1. Comprehension

（1）B

（2）B

（3）C

2. Learning about Language

（1）introduction

（2）preferred

（3）graduating

（4）determination

（5）Judging

Reading 2

1. Comprehension

Persons	Identity	What they did
Miss Chen	head teacher	organized us to climb Yunji Mountain and take pictures for the competition
Carol	monitor	set the schedule, arranged transportation and prepared prizes
Peter	classmate/student	won the competition but shared his prize with everyone
All students	/	packed up necessities, took the bus there, helped each other, successfully climbed to the top, sang and laughed along the way, took photos

2. Read the passage and answer the following question

The author thought this activity was meaningful and unforgettable because of their mutual help.

3. Learning about Language

(1) It was Tom who invited us to join in this trip.

(2) Even if nobody believes you can make it, you should be confident.

(3) My mother insisted that I (should) call her as soon as I arrived in Guangzhou.

(4) Once Tom makes up his mind, no one can change his mind except himself.

(5) I'm sure you will have fun talking with your friends at the party.

Unit 4 Cultural Relics in Xinfeng

Reading 1

1. Comprehension

(1) According to the passage, what does "complicated" mean?

A. complex

B. rapid

C. easy

D. difficult

(2) Which of the following is not the significance of the engraving of Zhangtian Mooncake Mould?

A. To strengthen the sense of self-identity.

B. To strengthen the sense of belonging.

C. To express the values of laboring people.

D. To expect safety, reunion and affluence.

(3) According to the passage, what is TRUE about a Dandingjiu?

A. People go there in order to drink wine.

B. There are five simple stages in a Dandingjiu.

C. It was used to encourage their families to give birth to boy babies.

D. All the people around here are often unwilling to rush for the offerings.

2. Translation

(1) 听她说话的口气她好像亲眼观看过担丁酒。

(2) 无论我们走到哪儿，我们都会找到新丰肠粉店。

（3）不是所有的图案都用来雕刻在饼印上。

（4）这些程序太复杂了，我记不住。

（5）我决定买一顶“得麻”留作纪念。

3. Fill in the blank

be to blame	frighten	burst out doing	because of	take measures

（1）Two players are out of the team ________ injuries.

（2）My personal judgment is that he ________.

（3）His ________ eyes made the boy feel________.

（4）As she was talking, the old man ________ （cry） with excitement.

（5）Our government is ________ to rescue those people.

Reading 2

Answer the questions.

1. Who is the interviewer and who is the interviewee?

2. How many steps are there in the procedure of making a “Dema”? What are they? Show them with some concrete things.

3. Do you think the “Dema” is worth 25 *yuan*? Why?

附参考答案：

Unit 4　Cultural Relics in Xinfeng

Reading1

1. Comprehension

（1）A

（2）D

（3）C

2. Translation

(1) It seemed as if she had watched Dandingjiu in person.

(2) Everywhere we go, we can find a Xinfeng Chang Fen reataurant.

(3) Not all patterns are used to be engraved on the mooncake moulds.

(4) These procedures are too complicated for me to keep them in mind.

(5) I make up my mind to buy a "Dema" as a memory.

3. Fill in the blank

(1) because of

(2) is to blame

(3) frightening; frightened

(4) burst out crying

(5) taking measures

Reading 2

Answer the questions.

1. Li Hua is the interviewer and the old lady is the interviewee.

2. The banboos used should be more than three years old. Then cut out the two ends of the banboos to get the middle parts and cut them into thin peels and weave. After covering them with some soft bamboo leaves and cement paper, people need to oid and dry them to make it a "Dema".

3. Open question.

Unit 5 Xinfeng Celebrities

Reading 1

1. Choose a word from the box to fill in the blank

join	guidance	base	devote	selfless	quality

(1) Activities all take place under the ________ of an experienced tutor (导师).

(2) Do you mind if I ________ you for lunch this afternoon?

(3) The company has its ________ in New York, and branches all over the world.

(4) The comrade Lei Feng is known as a ________ person, who always did good things for people without asking for any return.

(5) When costs are cut, product ________ suffers.

(6) I could only ________ two hours a day to work, because I have to spend most of the time taking care of my son.

2. Complete the passage according to the reading passage

Li Renyu was (1) ________ (birth) into a poor family. Because of his mother's (2) ________ (die) when he was a little kid, he had got to spend his childhood in his grandfather's house.Supported by his uncle, he was (3) ________ (send) to Guangzhou for study. Influenced by the thoughts about revolutionary, he (4) ________ (join) the Communist Party. In December,1927, he （5） ________ （take） part in Guangzhou Uprising. Later, he led an army to tightly unite the populace under the （6） ________ （guide） of the Fourth Red Army. On September 30th, 1932, he went to Baoding （7） ________ （secret）. However he was betrayed and captured. He suffered （8） ________ extremely severe torture in jail, but he never gave in. He made up his mind to devote （9） ________ （he） to the revolution and he really （10） ________ （do） it.

Reading 2

1. Put the following events in order

A. I arrived at the entrance of the village.

B. Uncle Paul was swallowed by fire.

C. I was dragged by Uncle Huang to the edge of a mountain.

D. A village turned to village cadres for help to deal with the mountain fire.

E. A strong wind blew and the fire came to life again.

F. Three village cadres including Uncle Paul rushed to the fire scene to rescue.

G. Uncle Huang and another cadre rushed into the fire sea to rescue Uncle Paul.

H. Uncle Paul never came to himself forever.

2. What are your feelings after you read this story?

3. Translation

（1）他是第一个因救人于火海而牺牲的英雄。

（2）只有在那时人们才明白生命的短暂。

（3）第一次单独和我叔叔在一起聊天时，我感到开心又害怕。

4. Grammar Filling

（1）Monica is a ________ （devote） friend. His ________ to us is quite clear.

（2）They believed that all men and women were born ________ （equal）.

（3）You should turn to your teacher for help when you meet with ________ （difficult） at school.

（4）She rewarded him ________ a smile.

附参考答案：

Unit 5 Xinfeng Celebrities

Reading 1

1. Choose a word from the box to fill in the blank

(1) guidance

(2) join

(3) base

(4) selfless

(5) quality

(6) devote

2. Complete the passage according to the reading passage

(1) born

(2) death

(3) sent

(4) joined

(5) took

(6) guidance

(7) secretly

(8) from

(9) himself

(10) did

Reading 2

1. Put the following events in order

DFEBGHAC

2.What is your feelings after you read this story?

Open question.

3. Translation

(1) He is the first hero to sacrifice because of rescuing people from fire.

(2) Only then did people realize the brevity of life.

(3) The first time I chatted with my uncle alone, I felt happy and scared.

4. Grammar Filling

(1) devoted; devotion

(2) equal

(3) difficulties

(4) with

第二辑

教学设计

Unit 1 Brief Introduction to Xinfeng 微课教学设计

表2-1 Unit 1 Brief Introduction to Xinfeng 微课教学设计表

<table>
<tr><td>授课教师姓名</td><td>李细娟</td><td>微课名称</td><td colspan="3">《“丰”味英语》Unit 1 Reading 1
—Brief Introduction to Xinfeng</td></tr>
<tr><td>学科</td><td>英语</td><td>视频长度</td><td>9分30秒</td><td>录制时间</td><td>2020年1月</td></tr>
<tr><td>教学类型</td><td colspan="5">讲授型、任务型</td></tr>
<tr><td>授课对象</td><td colspan="5">高二（11）班</td></tr>
<tr><td>主题语境</td><td colspan="5">人与自然</td></tr>
<tr><td>文本分析</td><td colspan="5">本土特色英语教程的开发，由学校教师调查研究后合作编写，贴近学生实际生活，立足当地，既有利于学生接触到符合当地学情的教材，也有利于培养学生的家乡情怀和文化，进而培养学生的中国情怀和文化自信。《“丰”味英语》校本课程以英语学科核心素养为导向，以新丰本土文化为载体，以用英语推广新丰文化为目标，使学生更多地了解新丰文化，培养学生在实际生活中应用英语介绍新丰的能力，并提升学生对本土文化和自身身份的自信</td></tr>
<tr><td>教学目标</td><td colspan="5">1.培养学生的语言能力、文化意识、思维品质和学习能力。
2.在发展学生英语语言运用能力的过程中，帮助学生理解和鉴赏中外优秀文化，培养中国情怀，坚定文化自信。
3.学生能运用阅读策略理解文章</td></tr>
<tr><td>学习者特征分析</td><td colspan="5">高二的学生具有比较系统的语言学习能力，对语言的人文性和工具性的统一也有了一定的理解。学生能在自主学习、合作学习、探究学习等过程中提升运用英语的能力，同时坚定文化自信，培养家国情怀</td></tr>
<tr><td>教学重难点分析</td><td colspan="5">教学重点：
1. 文本的理解和应用。
2. 通过文本阅读，过渡到应用文的写作。
教学难点：
英语宣传海报的制作</td></tr>
</table>

续 表

<table>
<tr><th colspan="3">教学过程</th></tr>
<tr><th colspan="2">内容</th><th>设计意图
核心素养提升点</th></tr>
<tr><td>Ⅰ. Lead-in</td><td>Enjoy the beautiful scenery of Xinfeng</td><td>【设计意图】通过展示秀美新丰的图片，燃起学生对家乡的热爱，帮助学生快速进入阅读情境，有目的地进行文章阅读及分析。
【核心素养提升点】学习多模态的语言输入</td></tr>
<tr><td rowspan="2">Ⅱ. Reading and Reading Tasks</td><td>Task 1: Filling the blanks
Introduction of Xinfeng
<table><tr><td>Name</td><td></td></tr><tr><td>Location</td><td></td></tr><tr><td>Area</td><td></td></tr><tr><td>Population</td><td></td></tr><tr><td>Attractions</td><td></td></tr></table></td><td>【设计意图】通过简要阐述新丰的基本要素，帮助学生快速进入阅读情境，有目的地进行文章阅读。
【核心素养提升点】语言能力：综合运用语言进行表达</td></tr>
<tr><td>Task 2: Answer the questions
Is the writer satisfied with their trip to Xinfeng?
How do you know?
Find the clues in the passage
Keys:
1.We couldn't wait to witness their wonderful views, so we drove direct to our first stop...
2.The amazing scenery on both sides kept us spellbound, so we didn't even notice that we had arrived.
3.After experiencing the relaxing hot spring, we completely forgot the troubles that we were upset about</td><td>【设计意图】培养学生的阅读能力，有助于他们更快、更全面地掌握阅读的内容。
【核心素养提升点】语言能力和阅读能力提升</td></tr>
<tr><td>Ⅲ. Make a poster</td><td>If you work in a travel agency, please make a poster to attract more people to visit Xinfeng</td><td>【设计意图】体现语言的工具性，把语言运用到真实语境中</td></tr>
</table>

续 表

<table>
<tr><th colspan="2">教学过程</th><th></th></tr>
<tr><th colspan="2">内容</th><th>设计意图
核心素养提升点</th></tr>
<tr><td>Ⅲ. Make a poster</td><td></td><td>【核心素养提升点】发展学生在真实情境中的语言运用能力和学习能力</td></tr>
<tr><td>Ⅳ. Assignment</td><td>Shape the poster and show it to the next class</td><td></td></tr>
<tr><td>教学反思</td><td colspan="2">学生对本土文化阅读理解的兴趣较浓，对新丰的基本信息的获取比较容易。通过问题的设计，从回答问题中了解阅读的内容。通过阅读让学生制作有关新丰的海报。教师可以在课堂上先做一个范例，这样学生完成任务会更轻松些</td></tr>
</table>

Unit 2 The Source of Hakka Dialect Reading 1微课教学设计

表2-2 Unit 2 The Source of Hakka Dialect Reading 1微课教学设计表

<table>
<tr><td>学校</td><td>新丰县第一中学实验学校</td></tr>
<tr><td>教师</td><td>余优玲</td></tr>
<tr><td>Book</td><td>“丰”味英语</td></tr>
<tr><td>Location</td><td>Unit 2 The Source of Hakka Dialect Reading 1</td></tr>
<tr><td colspan="2">Analysis of the Teaching Material 教材分析</td></tr>
<tr><td colspan="2">Based on the knowledge that students have mastered, the first reading of Unit 2 leads students to Hakka Dialect. Though it's more of a general introduction to Hakka Dialect, it actually paves the way for students to get closer to the dialects in Xinfeng, which we are positive that will finally grow students' interest and pride in their hometown</td></tr>
<tr><td colspan="2">Analysis of the Students 学情分析</td></tr>
<tr><td colspan="2">Senior high school students have already learned words and expressions, and they have passion for something which is not rigid but vivid and related to their lives ,and they will be active when put in a well-set class. Also, they start to have the initial sense of identity and culture</td></tr>
<tr><td colspan="2">Teaching Objects 教学目标</td></tr>
<tr><td colspan="2">Knowledge Objectives:
1.To review the words and expressions from textbook;
2.To master something about Hakka Dialect, including history, features and so on;
3.To prepare for the learning of Reading 2, Unit 2.
Ability objectives:
1.To train Ss' listening, speaking, reading, writing and viewing skills;
2.To develop Ss' critical thinking ability</td></tr>
</table>

续 表

<table>
<tr><th colspan="5">Teaching Objects 教学目标</th></tr>
<tr><td colspan="5">Moral Objects:
1.To grow Ss' sense of identity and let them take pride in the local culture;
2.To guide Ss to be cooperative and supportive</td></tr>
<tr><th colspan="5">Teaching Key Points and Difficult Points 教学重点和难点</th></tr>
<tr><td colspan="5">Key Points:
1.Review the key words and expressions selected from the textbook;
2.Make Ss familiar with the history and features of Hakka Dialect, especially its differences from Mandarin.
Difficult Points:
1.How to better illustrate the differences between Mandarin and Hakka Dialect;
2.How to set this lesson well and connect the article to Ss' real life</td></tr>
<tr><th colspan="5">Teaching Methods 教学方法</th></tr>
<tr><td colspan="5">Task-based teaching method，Audio-visual teaching method, Group learning method</td></tr>
<tr><th colspan="5">Teaching Procedures 教学过程</th></tr>
<tr><th>Steps</th><th>Purposes</th><th>Teacher's Activities</th><th>Students' Activities</th><th>Means</th></tr>
<tr><td>Step 1
Warming up</td><td>1.To warm up the class.
2.To review important words and expressions.
3.To lead in the topic</td><td>1.Invite Ss to do an activity—exercise your neck.
2.Start a free talk.（2 questions and 1 guessing game about Hakka Dialects' meaning）
3.Raise a question to lead in reading</td><td>1.Join in the activity.
2.Join the free talk.（answer the questions and play the guessing game）
3.Answer the questions</td><td>Multimedia/activity/game</td></tr>
<tr><td>Step 2
Skimming</td><td>1.To help Ss master the main idea of the article.
2.To train skimming skill</td><td>1.Guide Ss to skim the article by words.
2.Present Ss 3 questions to think.
3.Lead Ss to figure out the answers to the 3 questions</td><td>1.Listen to T.
2.Read 3 questions presented by T.
3.Skim the article.
4.Volunteer to answer questions</td><td>Multimedia/picture</td></tr>
</table>

续 表

Teaching Procedures 教学过程				
Steps	Purposes	Teacher's Activities	Students' Activities	Means
Step 3 Careful reading	1.To help Ss master detailed information of the article. 2.To train Ss' careful reading skill	1.Guide Ss to do careful reading. 2.Lead Ss to finish Activity 1—filling in the blanks. 3.Show 3 short videos of *Talking Cat Tom* speaking dialects and Mandarin, lead Ss to finish activity 2	1.Read the article carefully. 2.Compete to fill in the blanks by raising hands. 3.Watch the videos and match them with explanations	Multimedia/ different tasks of exercise/ videos
Step 4 After reading (Show time)	1.To help Ss retell the article by reading mind map. 2.To develop Ss' cooperation skill	1.Explain show time rules. 2.Emphasize a show is needed in the presentation. 3.Present the mind map and guide Ss to read it. 4.Organize Ss to practice retelling in group and assist. 5.Pick groups to check	1.Listen to the rules. 2.Follow T to read the mind map. 3.Practice in their groups. 4.Compete to do the presentation and show	Multimedia/ mind map
Step 5 Conclusion	Help Ss review what we have learned	Presents the major points and review with Ss together	Look at the major points and follow T to review	Multimedia
Step 6 Homework	1.Train Ss' writing skill. 2.Get Ss to think about local dialects critically	1.Present Ss the writing materials. 2.Explain the writing to Ss	1.Analyze the writing materials. 2.Listen to the T's explanation	Multimedia
Step 7 Self-assessment	To collect the feedback to improve teaching	1.Hand out the self-assessment paper. 2.Organize Ss to complete	Complete the assessment paper and hand in	Assessment paper

续 表

Blackboard Design 板书设计

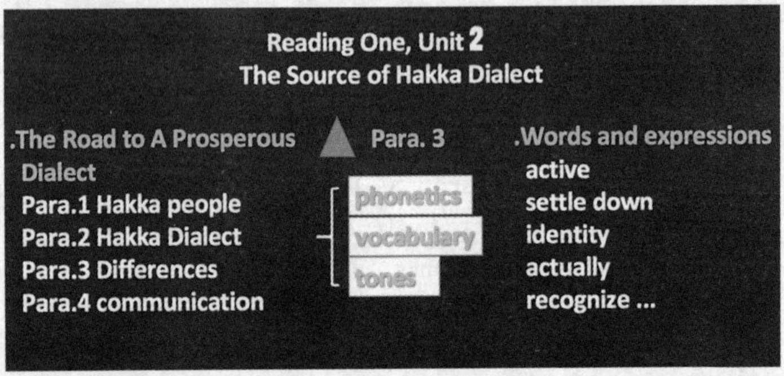

Teaching Reflection 教学反思

This lesson is well organized and divided into 7 steps in total. It starts with warming up with 2 activities, which warm up the class effectively.Next,it manages to deal with the reading step by step, including skimming, careful reading and after reading.During the course, students are required to take different tasks whose level increase gradually. Also, students are asked to write a short passage of their local dialects as homework, which greatly develops their critical thinking ability.

However, to be a qualified lesson designer, I should do more work to get students better involved in the lesson, making them the real masters of the lesson

附：

Self-assessment paper

Chinese Name: ________ English Name: ________ School NO. ________

Items （项目）	Excellent	Good	OK	Note （备注）
1.How well do you master the key words and expressions?				
2.How well do you understand the reading?				
3.How well do you perform in the group?				
4.How well do you perform in class?				
General comment to yourself:				

Unit 3 Xinfeng River Listening and Speaking微课教学设计

表2–3 Unit 3 Xinfeng River Listening and Speaking微课教学设计表

<table>
<tr><td>授课教师姓名</td><td>谭玉琳</td><td>微课名称</td><td colspan="3">《“丰”味英语》Unit 3 Listening and Speaking : Lugu River National Wetland Park</td></tr>
<tr><td>学科</td><td>英语</td><td>视频长度</td><td>15分21秒</td><td>录制时间</td><td>2020年4月</td></tr>
<tr><td>教学类型</td><td colspan="5">任务型</td></tr>
<tr><td>适用对象</td><td colspan="5">高一学生</td></tr>
<tr><td>设计思路</td><td colspan="5">本节是本单元第一课时的听说微课，以鲁古河为听说内容的载体，通过听说任务提高学生的听力理解能力和口头模仿能力。热身部分从中国的著名河流过渡到新丰的新丰江和鲁古河，在听文段之前教师先让学生进行单个单词或短语的听力匹配练习，旨在让学生熟悉较陌生的词汇，为听文段做准备。听文段后有两个任务：回答问题和听数字，既有泛听又有精听。通过引导学生熟悉听力中的关联词和数字，使学生掌握听力发展的线索。说英语的任务是高考题型的模仿朗读。广东新高考的听说分值增多5分，有必要在平时的练习中强化学生对题型的理解和熟悉度。为了让学生能够自主使用该微课，按照高考听说的步骤，提示学生停下，练习一分钟，再听一分钟，最后用手机录下自己的录音以检查学习效果</td></tr>
<tr><td colspan="6">教学过程</td></tr>
<tr><td colspan="4">内容</td><td colspan="2">时间</td></tr>
<tr><td>Ⅰ. Lead-in</td><td colspan="3">Step 1: Talk about some famous rivers in China and in Xinfeng County.
Aims: To get students familiar with famous rivers in China and then focus their attention on Xinfeng River and Lugu River in Xinfeng County, Shaoguan City</td><td colspan="2">2 minutes</td></tr>
</table>

续 表

<table>
<tr><th colspan="3">教学过程</th></tr>
<tr><th colspan="2">内容</th><th>时间</th></tr>
<tr><td>Ⅰ. Lead-in</td><td>Step 2: Introduce Lugu River briefly by three pictures.
Aims: To give students some background information about Lugu River in its geography</td><td></td></tr>
<tr><td>Ⅱ.Listening Tasks</td><td>Task 1: Listen and match the number and their Chinese meanings.
1 国家林业和草原局 6
2 水库 5
3 交叉点 2
4 保护、保存 1
5 公顷 4
6 复合的 3
7 亚热带的 8
8 二级支流 12
9 北回归线 11
10 地势 7
11 波浪起伏的 9
12 垂直的 10
13 水平的 13
14 特征 16
15 丰富的 14
16 维管植物 18
17 脊椎动物 17
18 生物多样性 15
Aims: To help students get familiar with the meanings of the difficult words or phrases that will appear in the following listening text.
Task 2: Watch the video and answer two questions.
1.When was Lugu River National Wetland Park of Guangdong built?
2. How many parts does Lugu River National Wetland Park include? What are they?
Answers:
1. It was built in December 2014</td><td>7 minutes 35 seconds</td></tr>
</table>

续 表

<table>
<tr><th colspan="3">教学过程</th></tr>
<tr><th colspan="2">内容</th><th>时间</th></tr>
<tr><td>Ⅱ.Listening Tasks</td><td>2. Seven. Lugu River National Wetland Park includes the rivers of its upper reaches, the Lugu River Reservoir, the lower reaches and their intersection with Xinfeng River, the dam on the Lugu River, the river stream and the surrounding water source conservation forest.
Aims: To get the detailed information by listening extensively.
Task 3: Listen to part of the video again and fill in the blanks with numbers.
The total planned area of the park is ________ hectares, and the total wetland area is ________ hectares with a wetland rate of ________. There are abundant species of wild animals and plants in the park, including ________ species of vascular plants and ________ species of wild vertebrates.
Answers: 469.54; 153.46; 32.68%; 1,208; 438.
Aims: To improve students' ability to get the numbers in listening</td><td>7 minutes 35 seconds</td></tr>
<tr><td>Ⅲ. Speaking Task</td><td>Step 1: Watch the video once about the introduction to Lugu River National Wetland Park.
Step 2: Now read the text of the listening by yourself. You are suggested to pause for 1.5 minutes to practise.
Step 3: Listen again and read after the recording.
Step 4: Read aloud by yourself to dub for the video.
Aims: To offer students an opportunity to get familiar with the steps of "Read aloud"</td><td>7 minutes 46 seconds</td></tr>
<tr><td>教学反思</td><td colspan="2">本次听说微课任务设计较为合理，课堂指令清晰，图文并茂。首先，从听单词到听文段，从泛听到精听，从听力输入到口语输出，层层递进，让学生逐步进入状态。其次，从介绍中国著名河流转向新丰的新丰江和鲁古河；通过讲解关于鲁古河的图片，激发学生进一步探索鲁古河的兴趣，为听说任务做好了铺垫；带领学生关注听说中的难词，学生能够自主按步骤学习该听说微课。学完该微课后，学生能积累与鲁古河相关的听力词汇，并且更加熟悉高考听说流程。
该微课可在以下方面改进：为使微课说的部分的模仿朗读更加连贯、真实，应制作模仿高考听说的模式连贯的听说视频</td></tr>
</table>

Unit 3 Xinfeng River Reading 1
微课教学设计

表2–4 Unit 3 Xinfeng River Reading 1 微课教学设计表

授课教师姓名	谭玉琳	微课名称	《"丰"味英语》Unit 3 Reading One —Xinfeng River		
学科	英语	视频长度	8分20秒	录制时间	2020年5月
教学类型	讲授型、任务型				
适用对象	高一学生				
设计思路	本次阅读微课是以新丰和新丰江为内容载体的演讲稿文本阅读。学生熟知新丰的知识，但是对新丰的英文表达积累欠缺，同时学生对演讲稿的体裁比较陌生。本次阅读课重在通过阅读任务积累新丰和新丰江的相关词汇，提高学生的阅读概括能力和理解能力，并在阅读和讨论中增强学生的家乡情怀，引导学生发现演讲稿的优点和缺点，辩证地看待各种宣传方式				
教学过程					
	内容				时间
Ⅰ. Lead-in	Step 1: Talk about two important rivers in Xinfeng—Lugu River and Xinfeng River. Aims: To get students familiar with the rivers in Xinfeng. Xinfeng River in particular. Step 2: Discuss some methods to advertise for Xinfeng River, including writing a letter, having a conversation and giving a speech. Aims: To lead students to think about the characteristics of some ways to advertise				2 minutes 20 seconds

续 表

<table>
<tr><th colspan="3">教学过程</th></tr>
<tr><th colspan="2">内容</th><th>时间</th></tr>
<tr><td rowspan="2">Ⅱ.Reading and Reading Tasks</td><td>Part 1: Reading time
Finish reading the four paragraphs, trying to satisfy the requirement of the reading speed in NMET.
Aims: To provide students with the opportunity to realize their gap between their reading speed and the required reading speed: at least 60 words per minute</td><td>50 seconds</td></tr>
<tr><td>Part 2: Reading Tasks
Task 1: Answer the questions.
1.What kind of genre（体裁） is this reading passage?
Answer: Speech.
2.Who is the author speaking to?
Answer: His or her fellows and judges.
3.Is the author taking part in a competition? Why?
Answer: Yes. Because he or she is speaking to the judges.
Aims: To get the basic information on the writing style by fast reading.
Task 2: Read the passage quickly and match the main idea of each paragraph.
Paragraph 1 is the introduction to the theme of the speech.
Paragraph 2 is telling that Xinfeng is a good place to travel.
Paragraph 3 is the introduction to Xinfeng River.
Paragraph 4 is about everyone's duty and the author's invitation.
Aims: To get the main idea of each paragraph and develop students' ability to summarize.
Task 3: Read the passage carefully and choose the correct answer.
Question 1: What does the underlined word “promising” mean in paragraph 2?
Answer: “Promising” means “possible and excellent.”
Question 2: Which of the following statements is correct according to the passage?
Answer: There is a hydropower station in Xinfeng County.
Question three: What's the author's purpose in giving this speech?
Answer: To attract tourists and call for protection.
Aims: To get the detailed information and train students' ability to infer</td><td>3 minutes 15 seconds</td></tr>
</table>

续 表

教学过程		
内容		时间
Ⅲ. Post-reading	Discussion: For advertising, what are the advantages and disadvantages of speech? Advantages: 1.The speaker can talk to many people at one time. 2.The audience can feel our emotions directly. 3.The speaker can see the audiences' reactions immediately. Disadvantages: 1.There is a lack of personal communication. 2.It is hard to get feedback from the audience , later... 3.Suggestion: Combine some methods of advertisements	1 minute 35 seconds
教学反思	本阅读微课流程较为顺畅连贯，学生对本土文化系列阅读理解的兴趣较浓，学生具备的新丰背景知识降低了阅读难度，使得本次阅读微课能集中地加强训练阅读方法和关注阅读体裁。从介绍鲁古河和新丰江引入限定时间文本阅读，读后通过做题增强学生的阅读能力，检验学生的阅读理解程度。同时，该阅读微课形式稍单调，讲授方式稍传统，可以开发多模态阅读资源，以使课堂教学更生动	

Unit 3 Xinfeng River Reading 2 微课教学设计

表2–5 Unit 3 Xinfeng River Reading 2微课教学设计表

授课教师姓名	谭玉琳	微课名称	《“丰”味英语》Unit 3 Reading Two — “Journey to Yunji Mountain”		
学科	英语	视频长度	9分12秒	录制时间	2020年5月
教学类型	讲授型 任务型				
适用对象	高一学生				
设计思路	本节是本单元的第二次阅读微课，是以云髻山旅游为内容的日记体裁文本。经过前面的听说课和阅读一微课，学生掌握了一定量的相关词汇，能用英语介绍新丰的部分景点，兴趣越加浓厚。本次阅读课通过阅读任务积累云髻山的相关词汇，提高学生对记叙文六要素的归纳能力，重在引导学生发现关注记叙文的人和事情，掌握事情发展的线索，从而形成初步的文章大意概括能力，最后在翻译练习中增强学生对高中重点表达短语和句型的掌握。另外，日记属于应用文文体之一，是新高考的作文考查形式，学生对日记体裁比较熟悉，日常日记的经验能起到正迁移的作用				
教学过程					
	内容				时间
Ⅰ.Lead-in	Step 1: Talk about some famous mountains in Guangdong Province. Aims: To get students familiar with famous mountains in Guangdong Province and then focus their attention on Yunji Mountain in Xinfeng County, Shaoguan City. Step 2: Introduce Yunji Mountain briefly and share one of the well-known legends about Yunji Mountain. Aims: To get students interested in exploring more about Yunji Mountain				3 minutes 10 seconds

续 表

<table>
<tr><th colspan="3">教学过程</th></tr>
<tr><th colspan="2">内容</th><th>时间</th></tr>
<tr><td rowspan="2">Ⅱ.Reading and Reading Tasks</td><td>Part 1: Reading time
Finish reading the five paragraphs, trying to satisfy the requirement of the reading speed in NMET.
Aims: To provide students with the opportunity to improve their reading speed to meet the required reading speed: at least 60 words per minute</td><td>1 minute 5 seconds</td></tr>
<tr><td>Part 2: Reading Tasks
Task 1: Fill in the table about “Journey to Yunji Mountain”. Find out the identity of each person and what they did.
<table><tr><th>Persons</th><th>Identity</th><th>What they did</th></tr><tr><td>Miss Chen</td><td>head teacher</td><td>organized us to climb Yunji Mountain and take pictures for the competition</td></tr><tr><td>Carol</td><td>monitor</td><td>set the schedule, arranged transportation and prepared prizes</td></tr><tr><td>Peter</td><td>classmate/ student</td><td>won the competition but shared his prize with everyone</td></tr><tr><td>All students</td><td>/</td><td>packed up necessities, took the bus there, helped each other, successfully climbed to the top, sang and laughed along the way, took photos</td></tr></table>
Aims: To focus on the six elements in a narrative, who and what in particular, to get the main idea in fast reading.
Task 2: Answer two questions.
What did the author think of this activity?
Why did the author think so?
Reference answer: The author thought this activity was meaningful and unforgettable, because of their mutual help.
Aims: To pay attention to the details about emotions and to infer from details</td><td>1 minute 55 seconds</td></tr>
<tr><td>Ⅲ. Translation</td><td>Step 1: Figure out the useful expressions from the text.
1. 强调句式It is/was +被强调部分+that/who+剩余部分；
2. 即使（even if）；
3. 坚持要求（insist that...）；
4. 下定决心（make up one’s mind）；
5. 改变主意（change one’s mind）；
6. 开心地做某事（have fun doing sth.）。
Aims: To help students develop the habit of summing up some useful expressions from the reading material</td><td>3 minutes 2 seconds</td></tr>
</table>

续 表

<table>
<tr><th colspan="2">教学过程</th><th></th></tr>
<tr><th colspan="2">内容</th><th>时间</th></tr>
<tr><td>Ⅲ.
Translation</td><td>Step 2: Use the given expressions to translate these sentences.
1.正是Tom邀请我们去参加这次旅行的。
It was Tom that/who invited us to join in this trip.
2.即使没人相信你能做到，你也应该对自己有信心。
Even if nobody believes you can make it, you should be confident.
3.我妈妈坚持要求我一到广州就得打电话给她。
My mother insisted that I （should） call her as soon as I arrived in Guangzhou.
4.一旦汤姆下定决心，除了他自己，没有人能改变他的主意。
Once Tom makes up his mind, no one can change his mind except himself.
5.我相信你会在派对上与朋友们开心地聊天的。
I'm sure you will have fun talking with your friends at the party.
Aims: To develop students' ability to make the learned expressions into use</td><td></td></tr>
<tr><td>教学反思</td><td colspan="2">本次阅读二微课环节紧扣、连贯，从介绍广东名山转向介绍云髻山，图文并茂，有效地激起学生对云髻山的兴趣，为阅读做好了动机铺垫。教师建议学生进行限时阅读文本，边阅读边做笔记，阅读任务前有提示。读前教师提示学生注意关注记叙文的人和事，以把握事情主要发展线索，先回忆积累相关短语，提供了较好的脚手架，再练习翻译句子。
该微课可在以下方面改进：在微课开始前明确重点和难点，让学生在读前明确读后任务，提高阅读效率</td></tr>
</table>

Unit 3　Xinfeng River Writing 微课教学设计

表2-6　Unit 3 Xinfeng River Writing微课教学设计表

<table>
<tr><td>授课教师姓名</td><td>谭玉琳</td><td>微课名称</td><td colspan="3">《“丰”味英语》Unit 3 Writing：Speech</td></tr>
<tr><td>学科</td><td>英语</td><td>视频长度</td><td>8分13秒</td><td>录制时间</td><td>2020年6月</td></tr>
<tr><td>教学类型</td><td colspan="5">讲授型、任务型</td></tr>
<tr><td>适用对象</td><td colspan="5">高一学生</td></tr>
<tr><td>设计思路</td><td colspan="5">本节课是本单元最后一个课时的写作微课，是以秀田古树为内容的演讲稿写作。演讲稿也属于应用文文体之一，属于新高考的作文考查形式。在微课最开头明确该课的重点是掌握演讲稿的结构和写作方法，难点在于写出一份既自然又适宜的演讲稿。导入部分总结了本单元学习过的新丰景点，呼应阅读一的演讲体裁。通过讲授，了解写演讲稿的步骤：先审题，明确主题和时态，通过观察总结出演讲稿的结构，提醒使用连接词以使文章更加连贯。在写作任务部分进行写演讲稿的实操审题，给出相关的短语和范文模板，让学生有足够的语料进行独立写作。农村地区的学生在日常学习中缺少演讲的经验，因此，教师可在最后提供演讲中的非言语技巧</td></tr>
<tr><td colspan="6">教学过程</td></tr>
<tr><td colspan="5">内容</td><td>时间</td></tr>
<tr><td>Ⅰ. Lead-in</td><td colspan="4">Step 1: Review the attractions in Xinfeng, which have been mentioned in the former parts of this unit.
Aims: To remind students of their impressions of attractions in Xinfeng.
Step 2: Suppose you are going to participate in a competition to give a speech about Xiutian Ancient Tree.
Aims: To provide students with a real context in writing a speech</td><td>1 minute 55 seconds</td></tr>
</table>

续　表

教学过程		
	内容	时间
Ⅱ.Tips for writing a speech	Step 1: Make clear the basic requirements for writing a speech. 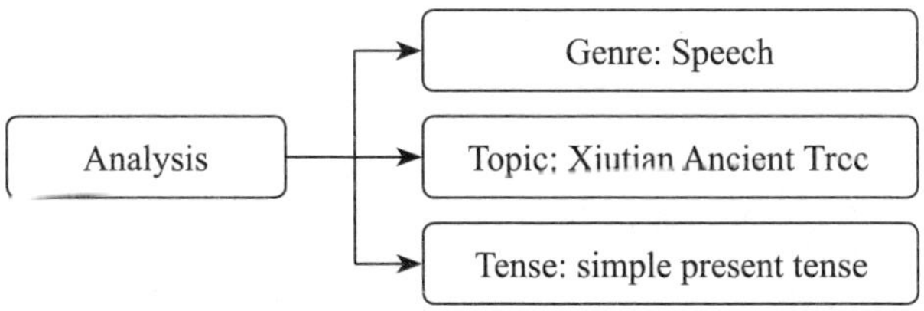 Aims: To remind students of the basic requirements to ensure basic correctness in writing a speech. Step 2: Analyze a sample to conclude the four parts of the structure of a speech. 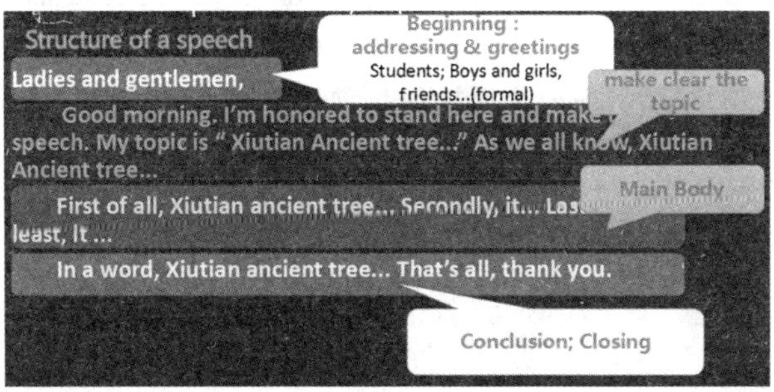 Aims: To master the structure of a speech. Step 3: Accumulate some linking words you'd better use in your writing. 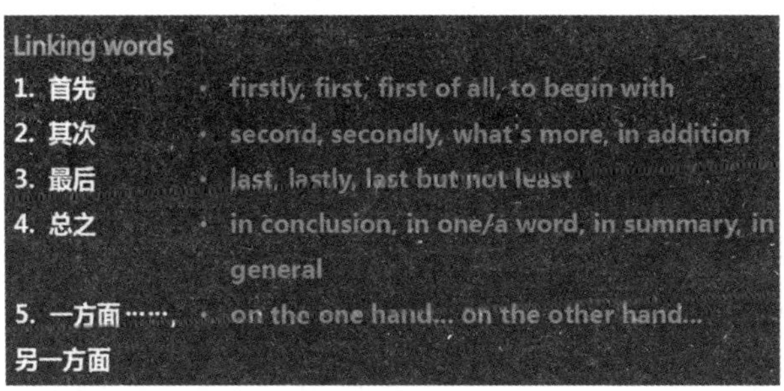 Aims: To remind students to use linking words to make the speech more coherent and well-organized	2 minutes 18 seconds

续 表

<table>
<tr><th colspan="3">教学过程</th></tr>
<tr><th colspan="2">内容</th><th>时间</th></tr>
<tr><td>Ⅲ. Writing task</td><td>Step 1: Read the details of the writing task and analyze by yourself.

假设你是李华。你将参加一次英语演讲比赛(Speech Contest), 主题是向外地人介绍秀田古树公园。请参照以下要点写一份演讲稿。
要点如下：
1.秀田古树公园位于新丰县马头镇，离县城十多千米。
2. 两棵四百多年历史的古秋枫树(Autumn maple)是那里的主要景点(Attraction)。古树保护区还包括绿地、园林(garden)、秋水湖等景观。
3.邀请大家过来游玩，感受新丰文化。
注意:
1. 词数100左右。
2. 可以适当增加细节，使行文连贯。

Aims: To let students practise the writing tips in carrying out the basic requirements and structure of a speech.
Step 2: Here are some related expressions about the contents of this speech.

Some useful expressions——phrases
1. 参加 · take part in/ participate in
2. 向某人介绍某物 · introduce sth. to sb.
3. 位于 · be located in/lie in
4. 离某地距离…… · ...away from sw.
5. 有400多年历史 · have a history of more than 400 years
6. 保护区 · protection zone/conservation area

Aims: To help students in finding out some useful expressions for their writing.
Step 3: Template of a speech about describing a place.

Ladies and gentlemen,
Good morning. My name is ______, ______ （明确身份）. It is my honor to be here to share my opinions on ____________ （提出话题）.
_______is located in _______, _______kilometers away from _______(地理位置). ________have a history of _________ （历史）. There are _____________ （景观）.
I sincerely invite all of you to travel here to enjoy ______(热情邀请). If you _____, I believe______(愿景). Thank you for listening(致谢)!

Aims: To offer students a template to write a standard speech if they don’t have their own idea</td><td>3 minutes 2 seconds</td></tr>
</table>

续 表

教学过程		
内容		时间
Ⅲ. Writing task	Step 4: Reference composition. Ladies and gentlemen, Good morning. My name is Irene. It is my great honor to introduce Xiutian Ancient Tree to you. Xiutian Ancient Tree is located in Matou Town, Xinfeng County, more than 10 kilometers away from the center of the county. The main attractions, two ancient autumn maple trees, have a history of more than 400 years. In the Xiutian Ancient Tree Park, we can appreciate varieties of views, including grass, gardens, lakes and so on. Besides, we can taste some delicious local food there. In a word, Xiutian Ancient Tree is a favorite worth visiting. I sincerely invite all of you to travel there and explore more about the local culture of Xinfeng. Thank you for your listening. Aims: To offer students a sample to memorize	4 minutes
教学反思	本次写作微课设计合理，从回忆本单元设计的新丰景点的内容到秀田古树，在内容上呼应了新丰景点，在形式上呼应了演讲体裁，让学生对本单元话题有整体的认知和掌握。在微课教学过程中，教师对演讲稿的写作步骤和结构进行了点拨，明确了基本的写作要求，提示学生运用关联词使文章更加紧凑连贯。在具体的写作任务中，教师让学生对提到的演讲稿写作技巧进行练习和强化，提供相关词汇和模板，降低了写作难度，增强了学生的写作信心。同时，教师教给学生的非言语技巧，能够让学生在日常学习生活中更加自然自信地完成一次演讲。最后该微课布置一个课后作业，让学生写完演讲稿后录制一个演讲视频，把演讲内容和演讲的身体语言结合起来，完成从输入到输出的过程，让写作任务更加真实	

Unit 4 Cultural Relics in Xinfeng Reading 1微课教学设计

表2–7 Unit 4 Cultural Relics in Xinfeng Reading 1微课教学设计表

授课教师姓名	陈娟丽	微课名称	《“丰”味英语》Unit 4 Reading One
学科	英语	微课时长	10分30秒
教学类型	讲授型 任务型		
适用对象	高一学生		
设计思路	本节课是本单元的第一篇阅读的微课，该文是以张田饼印和担丁酒为内容的采访体裁文本。本次阅读课通过Skimming, Scanning, Careful Reading, Summary和Homework五个步骤层层递进，旨在帮助学生了解采访体裁的特征，通过学习文章学生进一步了解本文两个本土文化遗产，增强学生的家乡情怀和文化自信。同时，通过练习和任务锻炼学生略读和寻读能力，以及通过思维导图总结概括的能力，进而提高学生的逻辑思维能力		
教学过程			
	内容		时间
Ⅰ. Skimming	Task 1: Skim the passage and answer the following questions. 1. What's the type of this passage? Aims: lead students to find out the features of the interview. 2. What's the main idea of this passage? Main idea （fill in the blanks）: This passage shows us an ________ between Li Hua, a high school student, and Mr. Pan, the general ________ of Bureau of Culture in Xinfeng. From the interview, we know two important cultural ________ in Xinfeng, nameed ________ and ________		3 minutes

续 表

教学过程		
内容		时间
Ⅰ.Skimming	Aims: Train students' ability to get the main idea of the passage quickly through the title and the topic sentence	3 minutes
Ⅱ.Scanning	Task 2: Scan and find all questions in the passage to know the details. （1） Can you introduce Zhangtian Mooncake Mould briefly to us? （2） How is a Zhangtian Mooncake Mould made? （3） Dandingjiu? Is it a kind of wine that we can drink? Aims: Lead students to know more about the procedures of making Zhangtian Mooncake Mould and the meanings of Dandingjiu, train students' reading comprehension skills, make students be more familiar with the local culture and enhance their cultural confidence	2 minutes 50 seconds
Ⅲ. Careful reading	Task 3: Choose the correct answers. 1.Which of the following is not the significance of the engraving of Zhangtian Mooncake Mould? A. To strengthen the sense of self-identity. B. To strengthen the sense of belonging. C. To praise the laboring people. D. To expect safety, reunion and affluence. 2. According to the passage, what is TRUE about Dandingjiu? A. People go there to drink wine. B. There are five simple stages in Dandingjiu. C. It was used to encourage their families to give birth to boy baby. D. All the people around here are unwilling to rush for the offerings. Aims: Check students' understanding of the passage and train their ability to locate the evidence in the passage through key-words in the questions	3 minutes

续 表

<table>
<tr><th colspan="3">教学过程</th></tr>
<tr><th colspan="2">内容</th><th>时间</th></tr>
<tr><td>Ⅳ.Summary</td><td>Task 4: Finish the following mind map about Zhangtian Mooncake Mould.
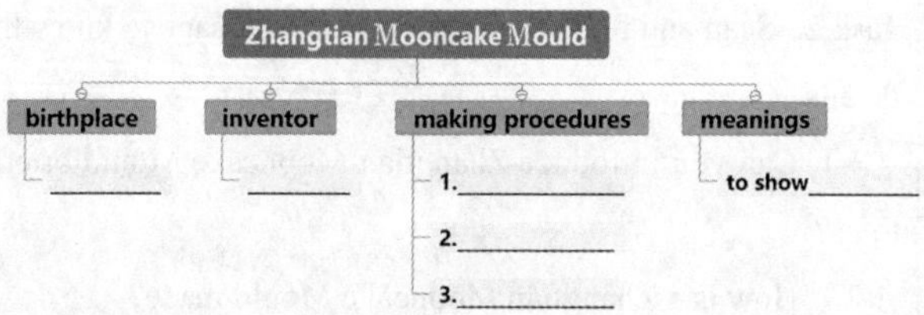

Aims: Train students' ability to summarize through the mind map and their logical thinking, review the knowledge about Zhangtian Mooncake Mould</td><td>1 minute 30 seconds</td></tr>
<tr><td>Ⅴ.Homework</td><td>Draw a mind map to introduce Dandingjiu to foreigners.
Aims: Lead students to review the knowledge about Dandingjiu by drawing a mind map to train their logical thinking</td><td>10 seconds</td></tr>
<tr><td>教学反思</td><td colspan="2">本次微课教学内容安排得当，层层递进，能较好地帮助学生了解张田饼印和担丁酒这两个本土文化遗产。课后作业是在Summary环节的基础上，让学生能学以致用，更有利于学生回顾本节课内容和提高画思维导图的能力。
该微课可在以下方面改进：Summary环节中思维导图的第二级内容可尝试让学生总结</td></tr>
</table>

Unit 4　Cultural Relics in Xinfeng Reading 2微课教学设计

表2-8　Unit 4 Cultural Relics in Xinfeng Reading 2微课教学设计

授课教师姓名	陈娟丽	微课名称	《“丰”味英语》Unit 4 Reading Two
学科	英语	微课时长	8分钟
教学类型	讲授型　任务型		
适用对象	高一学生		
设计思路	本节课是本单元的第二篇阅读的微课，该文是以新丰“得麻”为内容的采访体裁文本。本次阅读课通过Lead-in, Reading和Homework三个步骤循序渐进地引导学生学习新丰当地传统手艺“得麻”的相关信息，旨在帮助学生认识采访者与被采访者的不同，提高学生快速阅读的能力、对细节理解的能力和总结归纳的能力，引导学生揣摩作者的措辞，欣赏其语言之美，并通过读后讨论活动，引导学生形成正确的文化价值观，增强学生的家乡归属感、家乡情怀和文化自信		
教学过程			
	内容	时间	
Ⅰ.Lead-in	Can you name some Xinfeng specialties in English? Aims: Arouse students' interests in things that they are familiar with, lead students to recall some specialties in their hometown to enhance their sense of belonging to their hometown and cultural confidence, and train their ability to name local culture in English	1 minute	

续 表

<table>
<tr><th colspan="2">教学过程</th><th></th></tr>
<tr><th colspan="2">内容</th><th>时间</th></tr>
<tr><td>Ⅱ.Reading</td><td>Step 1: Fast reading
Task 1: Read the passage quickly and answer the following question.
Who is the interviewer and who is the interviewee?
Aims: Help students learn the differences between interviewer and interviewee.
Step 2: Careful reading
Task 2: Read the passage carefully and answer the following questions.
1.How many steps are there in the procedure of making a "Dema" ? What are they?
2.Why is "Dema" not selling well now?
3.Why did the author use "depressed" to describe Xinfeng "Dema" in the title?
Aims: Help students know more about "Dema" through these questions, train students' reading comprehension skills, lead them to think about the author's wording based on what they learned, get students more familiar with the local culture and enhance their cultural confidence.
Step 3: Post reading
Task 3: Fill in the following table and introduce "Dema" to foreigners
<table><tr><th>Name</th><th>Dema</th></tr><tr><td>function</td><td></td></tr><tr><td>material</td><td></td></tr><tr><td>price</td><td></td></tr><tr><td>current situation</td><td></td></tr></table>Aims: Lead students to summarize the information about "Dema" from different aspects and train their ability to summarize</td><td>6 minutes 30 seconds</td></tr>
</table>

续 表

<table>
<tr><th colspan="3">教学过程</th></tr>
<tr><th colspan="2">内容</th><th>时间</th></tr>
<tr><td>Ⅱ.Reading</td><td>Task 4: Group discussion
Do you think "Dema" should be passed on? Why or why not?
Aims: Lead students to discuss the meaning of cultural relics like "Dema", aiming at developing their sound cultural value</td><td></td></tr>
<tr><td>Ⅲ. Homework
(pair work)</td><td>Make an interview to introduce one specialty in Xinfeng.
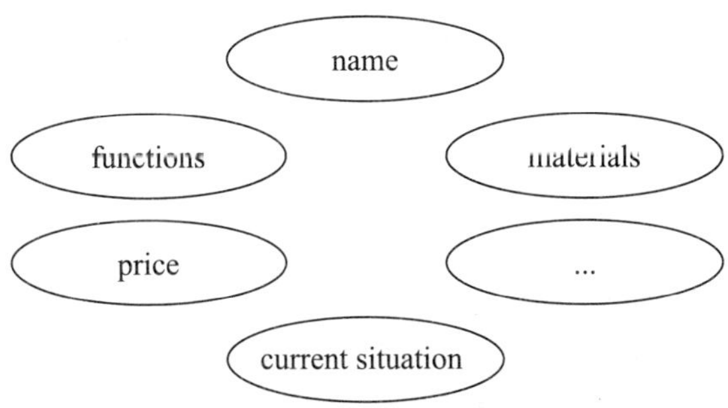

Aims: Check students' understanding of the features of the interview after learning this passage and lead them to learn more about the specialties in their hometown to enhance their sense of belonging and train their ability to introduce something in English</td><td>30 seconds</td></tr>
<tr><td>教学反思</td><td colspan="2">本次微课教学结构完整，层层递进，紧扣语篇主题，能较好地帮助学生了解"得麻"这个本土手艺。课后作业能呼应导入环节，并让学生运用本节课所学采访体裁模仿文章对话，介绍他们自己熟悉的当地特产，所有教学环节都能很好地为最后的作业输出做铺垫。
该微课设计可在以下方面改进：读后活动对于"得麻"的介绍在完成表格后，可让学生尝试写成小短文，更进一步提高学生的书面表达能力</td></tr>
</table>

Unit 5 Xinfeng Celebrities 1微课教学设计

表2–9 Unit 5 Xinfeng Celebrities 1微课教学设计表

<table>
<tr><td>授课教师姓名</td><td>余优玲</td><td>课程名称</td><td>《“丰”味英语》Unit 5 Xinfeng Celebrities</td></tr>
<tr><td>学科</td><td>英语</td><td>具体章节</td><td>Unit 5 Reading One</td></tr>
<tr><td>教学类型</td><td colspan="3">阅读课</td></tr>
<tr><td>适用对象</td><td colspan="3">高一学生</td></tr>
<tr><td>设计思路</td><td colspan="3">本单元的话题立足于新丰名人，本节课是本单元的第一篇阅读微课，通过导入和阅读两部分让学生主要了解新丰名人郑选民和革命烈士李任予的故事，且以后者为重。本节课从新丰名人引入，借助微视频介绍新丰近现代人物——郑选民；点亮学生的认知和兴趣后，通过对阅读文本的深入处理，让学生进一步了解另一名人——革命烈士李任予。在授课环节的活动设计中，教师既注重复习重点词汇与表达，提升学生的阅读和表达技巧，也注重课程思政，通过两位名人的故事灌输学生立德树人的理念和爱国爱家的精神</td></tr>
<tr><td colspan="4">教学过程</td></tr>
<tr><td colspan="3">内容</td><td>时间</td></tr>
<tr><td>Ⅰ.Lead-in</td><td colspan="2">Step 1: Recognize some present celebrities in Xinfeng and talk about them.
Aims: To arouse students’ interest in Xinfeng celebrities and get them participate in the class .
Step 2: Watch a video about Zheng Xuanmin, one of Xinfeng celebrities.
Aims: To shift students’ attention to the theme of this unit and get students to learn about Zheng Xuanmin</td><td>7 minutes</td></tr>
</table>

续 表

教学过程		
	内容	时间
Ⅱ.Reading	Part 1: Pre-reading Step 1: Present some pictures of "Nanmentang Square in Xinfeng." Aims: To attract students' attention and lead into Reading One—The Revolutionary Martyr—Li Renyu	2 minutes
	Part 2: Fast reading Step 1: Ask the students to fast read the article, select the best idea and determine the writing order of the article. Aims: To focus on the main idea in fast reading and teach students to tell order type applied in the article	5 minutes
	Part 3: Careful reading Step 1: Translate the sentences which include black words and phrases. Aims: To review the important words and phrases which need to be reemphasized. Step 2: Present 5 statements rephrased from the original text and ask the students to judge whether are true or false. Aims: To prepare students for better detail coping skills. Step 3: Complete the mind map related to the whole article. Aims: To better train students' reading skill by guiding them to focus on the details and learn to rephrase the expression as well	18 minutes
	Part 4: After reading Step 1: Organize the students to talk about the lesson they draw from Li Renyu in groups and a presentation is expected to be given in the next class. Aims: To provide the opportunity for students to have a discussion and be more cooperative; to guide them to think more deeply	5 minutes
Ⅲ. Conclusion and Self-assessment	Step 1: Lead the students to review the lesson by reading a flow chart. Aims: To help students do revision.	3 minutes

续 表

教学过程		
内容		时间
Ⅲ. Conclusion and Self-assessment	Step 2: Give out the self-assessment papers and assign the students to finish. Aims: To provide the students with a chance to reflect what they have learned and how well they have learned; to offer a chance for the teacher to vividly get the class reflection	
教学反思	本节微课设计环节环环相扣，每个步骤设计意图清晰、有条理。基于新丰名人的主题能有效地唤起且较好地维持学生的积极性。本节课在课堂的任务形式上也较灵活多变，既注重学生的知识技能，也强调情感技能和课程思政。 该微课设计可在以下方面改进：在授课时，若教师更加注重突出重点和难点，效果会更加良好	

Unit 5 Xinfeng Celebrities 2微课教学设计

表2-10 Unit 5 Xinfeng Celebrities 2微课教学设计表

<table>
<tr><td>授课教师姓名</td><td>余优玲</td><td>课程名称</td><td colspan="2">《“丰”味英语》Unit 5 Xinfeng Celebrities</td></tr>
<tr><td>学科</td><td>英语</td><td>具体章节</td><td colspan="2">Unit 5 Xinfeng Celebrities—Writing</td></tr>
<tr><td>教学类型</td><td colspan="4">写作课</td></tr>
<tr><td>适用对象</td><td colspan="4">高一学生</td></tr>
<tr><td>设计思路</td><td colspan="4">信件的书写是高中生英语写作的常见体裁之一。本节课的主要任务是重温书信的格式，教会学生书写感谢信。课程从温习书信的格式引入，以提问感谢信的书写目的为过渡，教师接着通过不同的课堂活动引导学生通过师生互动、生生合作共同完成写给篮球明星麦迪的感谢信，试图以讲授和实践相结合的方式来提升学生关于感谢信的写作技巧和技能</td></tr>
<tr><td colspan="5">教学过程</td></tr>
<tr><td colspan="4">内容</td><td>时间</td></tr>
<tr><td>Ⅰ.Lead-in</td><td colspan="3">Step 1: Present a letter and get the students to figure out each element of it.
Aims: To vividly review the structure of a letter and prepare the students for the next writing step.
Step 2: Ask the students to talk about the purpose of writing a letter of gratitude.
Aims: To shift students' attention to writing a letter of gratitude</td><td>3 minutes</td></tr>
<tr><td>Ⅱ.Writing</td><td colspan="3">Part 1: Prepare for writing
Step 1: Read the writing materials and underline the writing requirements with a red pen.
Aims: To get the students familiar with the writing requirements</td><td>6 minutes</td></tr>
</table>

续 表

教学过程		
内容		时间
Ⅱ.Writing	Step 2: Get students to draw an outline of this writing by working with a group, select the best version and rephrase it with the help of the teacher. Aims: To offer the students a chance to design how to cover writing points and set paragraphs.	
	Part 2: While-writing Step 1:Brainstorm the second part in groups: the changes brought by McGrady's funding, and give a presentation. Aims: To collect different thinking ideas from different students thus make the students realize the importance of thinking differently. Step 2: Lead the students to think and speak out the possible sentence structures of each writing point. Aims: To prepare students for writing from the sentence structure aspect and make them aware of the better expressions from their peers. Step 3: Complete the place mat to write a complete writing （a way to conduct writing in a small group: Each member is required to write on their own and stick what they write onto a paper given, choose the best version for each point together.） Aims: To get students to complete a complete composition and learn from each other	28 minutes
Ⅲ. Conclusion and Self-assessment	Step 1: Lead the students to review the writing procedures and the sentence structures applied in the article. Aims: To help students revise. Step 2: Ask the students to finish self-assessment papers. Aims: To help students reflect what they have learned and how well they have learned; to let the teacher vividly get the class reflection	3 minutes
教学反思	本节课开门见山，先以温习书信的格式引入，接着触发学生对感谢信写作目的的思考。教师通过画要求、列提纲等方式让学生掌握要点，以头脑风暴、快速说出写作句型、小组同写作进行比赛等形式进行写作，让学生在紧凑的活动中习得感谢信的书写。 该微课设计可在以下方面改进：在关注学困生的写作以及调动他们的积极性上还应该有进一步的思考	

第三辑

成果集锦

《课程情愫》读书摘录

新丰县第一中学　谭玉琳

一、丛书总序

“我们认为，品质课程是给予特定哲学而组织化的课程，是一种富有倾听感的课程，它将学生置于课程的价值原点，与学习需求匹配，努力在学生的学习需求和未来期待之间获得某种平衡的课程。”①

“众所周知，国家课程、地方课程、校本课程三类课程不是三个独立的部分，它们构成了学习课程的有机整体，用于共同的育人诉求，实现不同的课程价值，承担不同的课程任务，履行不同的课程职责，从不同的方面促进学生的成长与发展。”②

“我们应根据有关课程改革的精神，正确处理这三类课程的关系，保证各类课程的合理比例，充分体现三类课程对学生发展的综合价值，确保全面教育

① 崔春华，杨文斌.课程情愫：学校课程发展的另类维度［M］. 上海：华东师范大学出版社，2017：1.

② 崔春华，杨文斌.课程情愫：学校课程发展的另类维度［M］. 上海：华东师范大学出版社，2017：6.

质量观的落实。”①

二、目录

“通过从本地区民俗入手，挖掘中华优秀传统文化，并以传统民俗风情作为课程资源进行开发，既能使中华优秀传统文化焕发新的生命活力，还能使学校课程更加贴近人心，充分发挥课程潜在的文化感染力，培养学生的民族自信心、自豪感。”②

“优秀传统民间技艺是凝结了劳动人民智慧的文化瑰宝，它以各种特定的表现语言传达出中华传统文化的内涵和本质，体现着中华民族的审美爱好。民间技艺还蕴含着民族的社会深层心理以及哲学意涵，具有良好的温润人心的功能。”③

“非物质文化遗产是一种原生态的民族文化，它蕴藏着一个民族传统文化最深的根源，体现着一个民族特有的思维方式和升华方式。”④

三、前言

“本土文化是在一定地域内经一定的历史积淀下来的，它凝结着本土人民的智慧，也是一种独特的审美文化。课程，作为文化选择的一种工具，承担着本土文化传承的功能。将本土文化作为课程开发的重要资源，能让课程更亲

① 崔春华，杨文斌.课程情愫：学校课程发展的另类维度［M］. 上海：华东师范大学出版社，2017：6.

② 崔春华，杨文斌.课程情愫：学校课程发展的另类维度［M］. 上海：华东师范大学出版社，2017：1.

③ 崔春华，杨文斌.课程情愫：学校课程发展的另类维度［M］. 上海：华东师范大学出版社，2017：1.

④ 崔春华，杨文斌.课程情愫：学校课程发展的另类维度［M］. 上海：华东师范大学出版社，2017：2.

民，贴近人心，唤醒潜藏在学生内心的文化情愫。”①

“本土文化课程的开发应当以尊重差异、丰富体验、注重实践为基本理念。尊重差异，就是要尊重每一种本土文化间的差异；丰富体验，就是学校在进行课程开发时，应注重学生的文化体验，让学生在体验中了解本土文化，在体验中融入本土文化，成为传承本土文化的一分子；注重实践，就是要让学生掌握本土文化的实践技能，只有会操作、实践某一种本土文化才是真正地理解、接纳了本土文化。”②

四、提纲

第一章　乡土田园：孩子们内心深处的依恋

朝花夕拾课程：让每一个生命演绎童年的精彩

上海市嘉定区徐行小学，一所具有百年历史的农村老校。

1. 学校教育哲学：绿色教育（绿色发展论、绿色服务论、绿色育人论）。

2. 课程理念：让每一个生命演绎童年的精彩。

3. 课程愿景：追求学生、教师、学校的三赢发展。

4. 学校课程目标：“把‘仁爱、敏学、强体、特立’四个子目标进行细化分解，形成低、中、高三级段的课程目标”③。

5. 学校课程设置与课程实施：

红色道德圈——童心导航课程：生活体验内涵；

蓝色智慧圈——童智乐学课程：简单灵动开放；

绿色身心圈——童行健康课程：自信感悟全面；

---

① 崔春华，杨文斌.课程情愫：学校课程发展的另类维度［M］. 上海：华东师范大学出版社，2017：1.

② 崔春华，杨文斌.课程情愫：学校课程发展的另类维度［M］. 上海：华东师范大学出版社，2017：2.

③ 崔春华，杨文斌.课程情愫：学校课程发展的另类维度［M］. 上海：华东师范大学出版社，2017：8.

黄色个性圈——童性逐趣课程：综合经验实践。

新田园课程：让每一颗种子茁壮成长

上海市嘉定区曹王小学，地理位置较为偏远，外来务工子女占82%以上。

1. 学校课程哲学：新田园教育。“学校以‘新田园教育’为引领，着眼于新农村孩子的教育现实，缝合乡土发展与新农村人才成长的断裂，促进新农村优质教育均衡发展，努力打造一所特色鲜明的新农村优质学校。”①

2. 课程理念：让每一颗种子茁壮成长。“关注农村，关注儿童，关注生活，关注学生。”

3. 学校培养目标：“培养‘有梦想，会学习；亲乡土，会生活；爱科学，会探究；能生存，会合作’新农村娃。”②

4. 学校总体课程设置：基础课程、拓展型课程（生活课程）、探究型课程（发展课程）。

5. 具体课程和实施：

国家课程：“新田园课堂”行动；“新田园教师”行动。

校本课程：“新田园课程”基地（“丫丫农场”“记者站”“导游社”“种植队”“未来农业创想社”“果蔬创新栽培探究社”）；“新田园课程”学习方式。

6. 学校课程评价：“百香果奖”——曹王小学的最高荣誉，当学生或教师摘齐代表各自发展指数的花朵或果实时可获得③。

评价学生：“向日葵”“牵牛花”“君子兰”“太阳花”。

评价教师：“梅子”“桃子”“杏子”“李子”。

---

① 崔春华，杨文斌.课程情愫：学校课程发展的另类维度［M］. 上海：华东师范大学出版社，2017：23.

② 崔春华，杨文斌.课程情愫：学校课程发展的另类维度［M］. 上海：华东师范大学出版社，2017：25.

③ 崔春华，杨文斌.课程情愫：学校课程发展的另类维度［M］. 上海：华东师范大学出版社，2017：33.

领悟课程：为学会学习引路，为多元发展奠基

上海市嘉定区南翔中学，农村普通高中，1956年开始办学，传承了南翔古镇人敦本、尚善、崇文、践行的文化传统。

1. 学校课程哲学：

学校教育哲学——引悟教育

学校文化精神——敦本立人

学校课程理念——为学会学习引路，为多元发展奠基

“一流的教师、一流的课程、一流的管理、一流的文化是一流学校的四大核心要素。课程特色就是学校的办学特色。学校只有形成有特色的校本课程体系，才能凸显办学优势，才能满足学生个性发展的需求，才能实现提升学生综合素质的目标，才能全面提高教学办学质量。开发与建设校本课程，不仅是学习课程改革的突破口，也是打造学校办学特色、整体提升学校办学水平的着力点。”①

“校本课程是由学校全体教师、部分教师或者个别教师编制、实施和评价的课程，它使课程编制、课程实施和课程评价呈现’三位一体’的态势，具有了强大的优势。校本课程的开发是一种趋向，它能拓宽课程范围，适应个别差异，呈现最新动态，发挥创新意识。”②

2. 办学目标：打造个性鲜明的学校文化，创建富有特色的优质学校；激发每位学生的发展潜能，培育人格健全的合格公民。

3. 总的育人目标：培养“自律诚一、好学进取”的“有自信、守纪律、会学习、爱探索”的阳光少年，培养学生的自信心理、自主精神、自主意识和自创能力。

4. 课程目标：德育方面、智育方面、体育方面、美育方面、劳动方面。

---

① 崔春华，杨文斌.课程情愫：学校课程发展的另类维度［M］. 上海：华东师范大学出版社，2017：39.

② 同上。

5. 学校课程设置：

（1）基础型课程。

必修课程：①学科类基础课程；②学校特色课程。

（2）拓展型课程。

自主拓展课程：①学科类拓展课程；②德育校本化课程；③综合素养类课程。

限定拓展课程：①社团活动类课程；②实践体验类课程；③探究型课程。

必修课程——项目与课题研究：①学校指导型课题；②小组合作型课题；③个人攻关型课题。

（3）德育活动课程。

（4）社团课程。

（5）校园文化活动。

第二章 民俗风情：构筑贴心的精神家园

小鹤展翅课程：翩然鹤起 仰高树人

上海市嘉定区金鹤小学，创立于2008年，公办小学。

1. 学校教育哲学：仰高教育（“仰高”语出《诗经·小雅》：“高山仰止，景行行止。”）

2. 学校课程目标：旨在培养有追求的志气之少年、明是非的正气之少年、素养好的雅气之少年、活力强的灵气之少年。

3. 学校课程设置。

（1）育德课程：金小鹤实践行、金小鹤文明行、金小鹤安全行、金小鹤乐学行。

（2）育能课程：金小鹤人文行、金小鹤木偶行、金小鹤艺术行、金小鹤运动行、金小鹤思维行、金小鹤创意行。

4. 特色课程“妙手偶得”：“以木偶的制作与表演为主线，有机整合各学科的教育内容，从不同角度促进学生情感、态度、能力、知识、技能等方面的发展，凸显校园文化，发挥教师的特长，促进教师的专业成长。”[①]

一年级：手指偶；二年级：纸偶；三年级：布袋偶；四年级：提线木偶。

V-I-P课程：让每一个学生得到适切的成长

中光高级中学，创立于1945年，全日制公办普通高中。

1. 学校教育哲学：适合教育。“所谓‘适合教育’，是指关注个体差异，因材施教，促进学生个性发展和激发学生潜能的教育。适合教育把教育从应试的功利目光转向人的长远发展，注重个体内在生命力的激发，将‘以生为本’渗透到三个方面：从尊重个体差异入手，唤醒每个孩子的个性；靠近学生‘最近发展区’，激发个体生命潜能，提高创新能力；改变传统教育的评价体系，‘用多把尺子衡量学生’。”[②]

2. 学校课程目标：旨在培养“朴实、明理、进取、乐学”的学生品质，使他们具有“儒雅之气、刚柔兼备”的人文气质。

3. 学校课程体系：“V-I-P”课程结构。

V——课程（variety）：多样化选择课程。

I——课程（I）：个性化需求课程。

P——课程（primary）：基础性托底课程。

“V-I-P”课程体系涵盖“民族传统文化国学、文化艺术涵养、学生全面发展指导、绿色生态环保课程群”四大课程群，而这四大课程群又分别分布于学习的“V-I-P”课程的三大类课程中，涵盖修身养性、强健体魄、人文艺术、科技创新、生活技能五大方面。

① 崔春华，杨文斌.课程情愫：学校课程发展的另类维度［M］. 上海：华东师范大学出版社，2017：58.

② 崔春华，杨文斌.课程情愫：学校课程发展的另类维度［M］. 上海：华东师范大学出版社，2017：84.

第三章　民间技艺：温润每一个孩子的心灵

尚美课程：让“小龙人”踏着美的节奏成长

上海市嘉定区黄渡小学，创立于1905年，农村小学。

1. 学校教育哲学：尚美教育（尚美：崇尚美好）遵循儿童生长规律，顺应儿童天性。

2. 学校办学理念：向着美的方向生长。

3. 学校课程理念：让“小龙人”踏着美的节奏成长（“小龙人”形象工程，“小龙人”称号）。

4. 学校课程愿景：发展学生、发展教师、发展学校。

5. 学校课程目标：旨在通过“以美益德、以美启智、以美怡情、以美健体、以美促才”，培养“尚德、尚学、尚艺、尚格、尚新”的全面发展、个性鲜明、健康活泼的美丽“小龙人”。

6. 学校课程体系：“尚美”课程以“五力”课程结构为依托，将科学规范的基础性课程、自主合作的拓展性课程、个性选择的探究性课程分成五大类。

（1）崇尚道德之美（尚德）——“魅力”课程（提升个人魅力）。

（2）崇尚学习之美（尚德）——“实力”课程（激活智慧源泉）。

（3）崇尚艺术之美（尚艺）——“才力”课程（陶冶高雅情趣）。

（4）崇尚体格之美（尚格）——“活力”课程（练就健康体格）。

（5）崇尚创新之美（尚新）——“能力”课程（培养创新思维）。

7. 探索“寻美之旅”策略，全面推进校本课程的特色化实施。

（1）“三格”分层培养，提升师资素质：

① 三年内新老师的“入格”研修；

② 青年教师的“升格”研修；

③ 脱颖而出的教师的“风格”研修。

（2）“立体化”教研模式，提供坚实保障，双周五教研活动：“专题式”“沙龙式”“叙事式”等大型组教研活动；备课小组“课例式”研讨活动。

（3）“职级制”课堂管理，探索校本化实施。

HOME课程：看着每一个孩子的眼睛

上海市嘉定区马陆育才联合中学，创立于1957年。

1. 学校教育哲学：圆融教育。

圆融，可以寓意为永无止境的追求，没有最好，只有更好。

圆融教育，是尊重多元的教育。

圆融教育，是平等对话的教育。

圆融教育，是合作参与的教育。

圆融教育，是适性扬长的教育。

2. 课程理念：看着每一个孩子的眼睛，参与变得不可逃避，合作提升学习能力，差异成就个体发展。

3. 学校育人目标：培养“会学习，有潜力；勤健身，有韧劲；善合作，有梦想”的初中毕业生。

4. 学校课程体系：“同心圆”结构①。

圆心（蓝色）——以学生发展为核心。

内环（红色）——加德纳的多元智能：语言智能、数学逻辑智能、认识自然智能、身体运动智能、音乐智能、空间智能、人际关系智能、自我认识智能。

中环（绿色）——HOME特色课程体系（四大板块）：

H（Happy）——快乐，悦赏课程，提高学生的人文素养；

O（Open）——开放，拓思课程，改善学生的实践技能和思维方式；

ME（我）——show（秀才）课程，培养学生的兴趣，促进学生的个性成长；

HOME——家，乐家课程，完善学生的道德发展，培养合作能力。

“不同维度，教育意义融合；不同方法，课程目标融合；不同对象，课程

---

① 崔春华，杨文斌.课程情愫：学校课程发展的另类维度［M］. 上海：华东师范大学出版社，2017：113.

文化融合。”[①]

5.“圆桌教学”的理念与操作：

“1234合作探究”。

“1”—— 一个核心：以学定教。

“2”—— 两种课型：新授课和复习课。

“3”—— 三个“动”：动口、动手、动脑。

“4”—— 四个环节：探究导学、精讲助学、合作练学、检测反馈。

“合作”。

“探究”。

第四章 传统体育：磨砺孩子的进取品格

“我国传统民间体育具有独特的魅力，它具有贴近生活、喜闻乐见、老少皆宜的特点。此外，我国传统民间体育是基于博大精深的传统文化发展形成的，它不仅仅锻炼人的体魄，同时更专注于人的品行修养，其中还蕴含着拼搏、进取的民族精神。”[②]

暖记忆课程：用智慧启迪智慧，用温暖传递温暖

上海市嘉定区娄塘学校，地处嘉定工业园区，农村九年一贯制学校。

1. 学校课程理念：“暖记忆课程”。

“场景记忆是唯一能够把我们在时间上带回到‘过去’的记忆能力，它让我们回忆起过去某一时空的现实情境，让我们感到温暖。”[③]

“暖教育”，即组织、理解、赏识、激励学生，用真知、珍爱奠基每一个学生的美好人生。

---

① 崔春华，杨文斌.课程情愫：学校课程发展的另类维度［M］. 上海：华东师范大学出版社，2017：119.

② 崔春华，杨文斌.课程情愫：学校课程发展的另类维度［M］. 上海：华东师范大学出版社，2017：121.

③ 崔春华，杨文斌.课程情愫：学校课程发展的另类维度［M］. 上海：华东师范大学出版社，2017：124.

2. 学校课程总目标：旨在培养自爱、自信、自立、自强、会合作、懂感恩、具有爱国心的温暖学生。

3. 学校课程体系："七巧板框架"。

自爱课程——生活安全、自我保护。

自信课程——性别教育、快乐生活。

自立课程——食在娄塘、自理自立、生活理财。

自强课程——强身健体、经典朗读。

合作课程——追寻梦想、学科融合。

感恩课程——感恩父母、感恩师长、感恩自然、感恩社会。

爱国课程——古镇娄塘、魅力上海、大爱中国。

双"W"课程：让我们做得更好

上海市嘉定区徐行中学，初中学校，位于嘉定北郊徐行镇，创建于1958年。

1. 学校教育哲学：双"W"教育。"文"（WEN）以修心、"武"（WU）以健身，概括起来就是学生"人格"与"体格"并重的教育。培养学生"学习自主、道德自律、健体自觉、交往自如"的"四自"目标，培养体格强健、人格健全的合格初中毕业生。

2. 课程理念：让我们做得更好（学校课程内容、教师、学生）。

3. 学校课程体系：双"W"课程包含了学生、资源、教师三个层面的课程内涵，具体构建为"三环圆环环相扣"的结构。

（1）艺术人文课程（地方课程及学校特色教育课程）。

（2）基础、探究类课程（国家课程学科统整课程）。

（3）健身特色课程（健身特色课程，包括武术课程）：

① 基础型课程校本化；

② 拓展型课程弹性化（"统一+选择"的模式）；

② 探究型课程学校特色化。

第五章　非遗文化：血脉中流淌的自豪感

"非物质文化遗产是一种原生态的民族文化，它蕴藏着一个民族传统文化最深的根源，体现着一个民族特有的思维方式和升华方式。”①

GPS课程：让课程成为学生成长的阶梯

上海市嘉定区封浜高级中学，创办于1959年，生源质量不甚理想，家长重视程度不高，师生缺乏自信。

1. 学校课程理念：“一个孩子，一份选择”。

2. 学校课程目标：旨在培养善于动脑（Head）、勤于动手（Hand）、乐于用心（Heart）、勇于健康（Health）的和谐发展的“4H”学生。

3. 学校课程体系：点线面课程架构。

（1）挖掘资源点：四大类课程（学科1+X、人文素养、创意技艺、社会实践）。

（2）组成目标线：四模块（善用脑、勤动手、乐用心、勇健康）。

（3）拓展育人面：四整合（学科德育、活动平台、内外资源、综合评价）。

4. 学校课程模式：四大类、四模块、四整合的“GPS课程”模式。

在“GPS”模式中，G——Guided，指南的；P——Primary，基本的；S——Suitable，适合的。

5. 学校课程结构：

（1）基础型课程（学科基础型课程）。

（2）拓展型课程（学科拓展课程、综合类拓展课程、实践类拓展课程）。

（3）研究型课程。

6. 学校特色课程：

（1）德育课程。

（2）非遗课程。

7. 学校课程实施：

（1）基础型课程：打造“三心课堂”，关注学生学习方式的完善。

宏观理念：Positiveness（信心）；Patience（耐心）；Persistence（决心）。

---

① 崔春华，杨文斌.课程情愫：学校课程发展的另类维度［M］. 上海：华东师范大学出版社，2017：154.

中观诠释：H-O-P-E教学法（策略：低起点、小台阶、多活动、勤反馈）。

H——Habit：习惯改变；

O——Object：目标导向；

P——Progress：激励进步；

E——Exercise：练习设计。

微观操作：4G（Guide）助推，即导向、导读、导思、导习。

（2）拓展型课程：为学生自主选择、个性发展提供空间；明确主题，形成自主性拓展型课程教材，建立有效的管理机制。

（3）研究型课程：学研并重，努力培养学生创新素养和实践能力，重视学生科学素养培养；加强过程管理，抓好节点。

国韵课程：以“崇善·尚美·蕴思”为导向培养丰中阳光少年

上海市嘉定区丰庄中学，创办于1999年3月，外地生源多，学生家庭教育环境较差。

1. 学校办学理念：国韵丰中、德艺双馨、人文健康、和谐发展。

2. 学校课程分目标：培养学生的“国韵”艺术素养，培养学生的学科特长，弘扬健体的体育精神。

3. 学校课程体系：

① 基础型常态课程：根植于国家课程规划，培养适应未来社会、具有现代公民意识的建设者和接班人。

② 拓展型社团课程：科技类、语言与文化类、运动与健身类、艺术类。

③ 德育系列化课程：以情感教育为主线，形成贴近时代的德育课程；以养成教育为抓手，形成常态化德育课程；以专题教育为主轴，形成系列课程内容；把少年宫活动纳入重要课程平台。

④ 学校的课程资源。

注：该读书笔记为提纲式读书笔记。

教研论文

基于核心素养英语阅读教学活动中中国文化的渗透

新丰县第一中学 陈娟丽

本文围绕核心素养，以英语人教版必修模块为案例，探讨了如何在阅读教学活动中渗透中国文化，以培养学生的文化意识，使其获得文化知识，理解文化内涵，比较文化异同，汲取文化精华，具备一定的跨文化沟通和传播中华文化的能力。

一、在英语阅读教学中渗透中国文化的意义

（一）响应新课程标准要求

《普通高中英语课程标准（2017年版）》中提出，英语学科核心素养主要包括语言能力、文化意识、思维品质和学习能力。而“文化意识”指对中外文化的理解和对优秀文化的认同，是学生在全球化背景下表现出的跨文化认知、态度和行为取向。

《普通高中英语课程标准（2017年版）》的基本理念中提出，在发展学生英语语言运用能力的过程中，帮助他们学习、理解和鉴赏中外优秀文化，培育中国情怀，坚定文化自信，开阔国际视野，增进国际理解，逐步提升跨文化沟通能力、思辨能力、学习能力和创新能力，形成正确的世界观、人生观和价值观。

学科核心素养发展目标中的“文化意识目标”提出学生要获得文化知识，理解文化内涵，比较文化异同，汲取文化精华，具备一定的跨文化沟通和传播中华文化的能力。

综上所述，在英语教学中渗透中国文化符合新课程标准要求，是十分有必要的。

（二）消除中西沟通中的“中国文化失语症”

当下中学生乃至大学生仅限于“寒暄天气饭食”的“低级英语”交流，以及“无从深入下去”的“哑巴英语”。究其原因，其头脑中本国文化内容对应的英文表达，甚至本国文化内容的缺席应列其中。因此，在英语教学中渗透中国文化是消除这种中国文化失语症，实现真正意义上的交流沟通的必要途径。

二、中国文化在英语阅读教学中的现状

语言是文化的载体，是文化的一种表现形式，其自身也是一种文化现象。此外，语言具有工具性和文化性两种属性，这两种属性是相辅相成、不可分割的。但是在现实阅读教学中，由于教学成绩的压力，教师常常会将更多时间花在语言点、语法点、长难句和重点句型等的教授上，从而忽视文章所蕴含或可挖掘的文化内涵。这与新课程标准所提出的“核心素养”中的“文化意识目标”相违背。

曾有人统计过，人教版高中英语教科书中的英语文化内容高于本土文化内容一倍以上。也正因此，教师往往会忽视在英语教学中渗透优秀中国文化，而将重点放在向学生传授外国文化上。比如，在节日方面，很多英语教师有与学生一起过圣诞的习惯，却较少听闻有英语教师与学生一同过传统中国节日。其中反映出来的教师不重视中国文化的问题值得我们深思。

当然，随着“核心素养”的提出以及大家对其的深究，现今大家对英语教学中中国文化的渗透也越来越重视，这也是喜闻乐见的现象。例如，有学者推出“英语说中国文化”（Hello China）系列视频，用英语加动画惟妙惟肖地向世人介绍中国的特色文化，如中国功夫、太极拳、中医、农历等。又如“用英语讲好中国故事”系列视频，还可用英语介绍中国各城市的景色与特点。诸如

此类素材的涌现，既可以向世人更好地介绍中国文化，也有利于增强学生传播中华文化的能力，培养学生的文化意识，提高学生的文化自信，恰恰响应了新课程标准的要求。

三、在阅读教学活动中渗透中国文化的注意事项

（一）教师要深入分析教材文本

教材，对于学生的学和教师的教都起着重要的指导作用。因此，从教材入手，挖掘其文化内涵，是进行文化教学的首要选择。教师要对教材文本进行深入分析，找准切入口，充分利用教材文本进行中国文化渗透。本文选取英语人教版必修模块作为阅读文本素材进行分析。

（二）活动设计要紧扣文本主题

笔者认为，在阅读教学活动中渗透中国文化须在该阅读文本的主题基础上拓展或延伸，而不能完全脱离原阅读文本，否则会让学生觉得活动有些突兀，且容易造成学生的知识断层，从而使学生对活动无从下手、无话可说。

（三）活动设计要有的放矢

在阅读教学活动中渗透中国文化，不能只为了渗透而渗透，而应该依照新课程标准的要求，同时发展学生其他方面的素养（如语言能力、思维品质和学习能力），做到一举多得。

四、渗透中国文化的阅读教学活动设计与分析

本文选取英语人教版的必修模块作为阅读文本素材，根据活动展示方式将阅读教学活动分为海报、续写、思维导图、课堂问答、写信和辩论六种类型，每种类型设计一至两个渗透中国文化的教学活动，并围绕英语学科核心素养对这些活动进行分析。

（一）海报

海报这种活动形式可以分为小组或个人进行，是学生综合能力的一种展示。笔者比较主张以小组形式进行，可培养学生的团队合作精神。同时，海报的设计与排版等可以培养学生的动手能力与创新思维。

【活动1】必修三 Unit 2 Reading Two: Come and Eat Here（2）

教师可以通过以下读后活动渗透中国文化：

Suppose you have a chance to open your own Chinese restaurant now. Please design a poster to introduce your own menu to your group members. Make sure you high-light the advantages of your menu.

本单元的主题语境是“人与自我”中的“健康的生活方式、积极的生活态度”。通过本单元两篇阅读的学习，学生对健康饮食已有一定的了解。以上读后活动让学生以小组为单位为他们自己的中餐厅设计一个特殊的海报，重点要求学生突出其菜单的优势，旨在引导学生思考如何搭配出营养均衡的中式菜单，以培养学生健康饮食的意识，并提高学生对中式饮食的文化自信。同时，学生在设计海报时，通过翻译中式菜式的名字，既复习了该单元相关词汇表达，又能领略中英文化的异同，锻炼学生传播中华优秀文化的能力。

【活动2】必修四 Unit 2 Reading One: A Pioneer for All People

教师可以通过以下读后活动渗透中国文化：

According to the reading passage, please design a poster to introduce our pioneer Yuan Longping to foreigners. Make sure you add your own comments about Yuan on it, such as “What qualities have you learned from him?” and so on.

本单元的主题语境涵盖了“人与社会”中的“对社会有突出贡献的人物”和“人与自然”中的“自然科学研究成果”。通过该文本的学习，学生对袁隆平的一生与成就有了一定的了解，通过海报形式向外国人介绍中国科学家袁隆平，既可以巩固学生在该文本中获得的优秀中国精神文明知识，又可以提高学生的语言技能（理解性技能和表达性技能），并提高他们总结文本内容的逻辑思维能力。同时，学生通过向外国人介绍中国科学家这一过程，能坚定文化自信，逐步提升其跨文化沟通能力，并且通过总结袁隆平身上值得学习的专注研究水稻、无私帮助他国等优秀品质，增强学生的国家认同和家国情怀，同时逐步形成正确的世界观、人生观和价值观。

（二）续写

续写是新高考的趋势，对学生的写作能力要求较高。读后续写是结合阅读理解进行写作练习的一种方法。续写将语言输入与输出紧密结合，将语言的模仿性与创造性使用有机结合，将语言的学习与运用切实结合。续写是提高外语学习效率的好方法。所以，教师可以通过学生熟悉的教材文本着手渗透中国文化，同时锻炼了学生的续写能力。

【活动】必修一 Unit 3 Reading Two: Journey Down The Mekong（Part 2）

教师可以通过以下续写活动渗透中国文化：

Please continue the story by telling what happened after Wang Kun and Wang Wei met their cousins in Dali. The following contents should be included:

（1）The beautiful scenery they saw in Dali.

（2）They met some difficulties in Dali, but they overcame them with teamwork.

本单元的主题语境主要是“人与自然”中的“主要国家地理概况”，语篇类型是游记类的记叙文。通过本单元的学习，学生对游记的描写有了一定的了解，通过续写游记的方式可以提高学生应用所学的游记描写语言的技能；由于学生处于高一阶段，刚接触续写，所以通过两个指引性内容要求引导学生有的放矢。第一点内容是让学生描写大理的美丽风光，旨在引导学生鉴赏中国的优秀文化，培育学生的中国情怀；第二点内容是让学生设想一下他们途中遇到某些难题但最终通过合作，共同克服了困难，旨在帮助学生形成自强、合作和不畏艰难险阻的良好品格。

（三）思维导图

思维导图一种非常好用的思维工具，它可以帮助学生快速厘清思维、构建知识框架、提升思维能力和学习效率。

【活动】必修三 Unit 1 Reading One: Festivals and Celebrations

教师可以通过以下读后活动渗透中国文化：

（1）Please draw a mind map to summarize the festivals and celebrations introduced in the reading passage.

（2）According to what we have learned, can you draw another mind map to introduce your favorite Chinese festival to foreigners?

本单元的主题语境是“人与社会”中的“不同民族文化习俗与传统节日”，语篇类型是说明文。通过该文本的学习，学生对文中所介绍的世界各地几种类型的节日有了一定的了解，通过以上活动的第一步，可以让学生运用思维导图对文中各种节日的关系与介绍进行总结，从而使学生巩固所涉及的语言知识和文化知识，并提高学生归纳总结信息的能力；而活动的第二步则是在第一步的基础上，让学生模仿教材文本中介绍节日时所用语言与所涉及的信息，介绍他们自己最喜爱的中国节日，不仅可以锻炼学生的语言技能，而且可以引导学生更深入地了解中国优秀传统节日，增强学生的民族自信心与自豪感。

（四）课堂问答

课堂问答是课堂上常用的反馈较为快速、直接的活动形式，教师通过设计特定的问题引导学生思考讨论，以达到某种教学目的。

【活动1】必修一 Unit 2 Reading One: The Road to Modern English

教师可以通过以下问题渗透中国文化：

As time goes by, do you think Chinese English will develop its own identity? Why?（Group work: please discuss these questions with your group members）

本单元的主题语境是“人与社会”中的“社会进步与人类文明”，语篇类型是说明文。通过该文本的学习，学生对现代英语的发展史有了一定的了解，并了解世界上存在各式各样的英语。通过提问“随着时间的推移，中式英语是否会有自己的身份”，引导学生讨论和思考中西语言文化之间的差异以及相互之间的影响，既可锻炼学生的自我表达技能以及推理判断能力，又可促进学生形成跨文化意识，坚定其中国文化自信。

【活动2】必修二 Unit 2 Reading One: An Interview

教师可以通过以下问题渗透中国文化：

Why did Li Yan say it was a great responsibility but also a great honor to be chosen to host the Olympic Games? Take Beijing, for example, please list its responsibilities and honors to host the 2022 Winter Olympic Games.

本单元的主题语境是“人与社会”中的“体育活动、大型体育赛事、体育与健康、体育精神”，语篇类型是访谈。通过该文本的学习，学生了解了现代奥运会与古代奥运会的异同以及奥运会精神。通过提问“为什么李艳说主办奥运会既是一种责任也是一种荣耀”，并让学生以北京举办2022年冬奥会为例，列举出这次体育活动给北京赋予什么责任和荣誉，引导学生讨论和思考举办奥运会背后的意义，并在此过程中领略中国的国际责任感与荣誉感，从而坚定学生的中国文化自信，并提升他们的自豪感。

（五）写信

写信几乎是高考必考的形式，主要考查的是学生针对某一情境的交际能力，同时整合了语言知识、文化知识、语言技能等学习内容的考查。所以教师可以利用写信这一形式渗透中国文化，在培养学生文化意识的同时还能锻炼学生的书面交际能力。

【活动1】必修一 Unit 1 Reading One: Anne’s Best Friend

教师可以通过以下写信任务渗透中国文化：

作文题目：假如你是第二次世界大战时期的李华，请根据以下内容给Anne写一封100词左右的信。内容要求如下，可适当添加细节：

（1）读了她的日记，感同身受。

（2）告诉她中国第二次世界大战的情况，并表达中国最终会胜利的信心。

（3）希望能与她做朋友。

本单元的主题语境主要是“人与社会”中的“重大政治、历史事件，文化渊源”，语篇类型是写信。通过该文本的学习，学生了解了犹太人Anne在第二次世界大战期间的处境及其对自由的渴望。以上写信任务旨在培养学生的同理心，提高学生跨文化交流的能力，同时引导学生重温中国第二次世界大战时期的情况，使其铭记历史，增强其家国情怀，树立人类命运共同体意识。

【活动2】必修四 Unit 4 Reading One: Communication: No Problem?

教师可以通过以下写信任务渗透中国文化：

作文题目：假如你是李华，你的美国笔友Peter要到他的中国好友李明家做客，想知道中国的餐桌礼仪。请你写一篇100词左右的信件，告诉他如何就餐。内容要求如下，可适当添加细节：

（1）可以带一点小礼物以表示感谢。

（2）如何使用筷子，不能用筷子敲碗盘；放下筷子表示吃饱。

（3）如何婉拒某种食物。

本单元的主题语境涵盖了“人与社会”中的“跨文化沟通、包容与合作”和“不同民族文化习俗与传统节日”，语篇类型是记叙文。通过该文本的学习，学生了解了各国有着不同的肢体语言文化，为了避免交流中产生误会，学习和了解各国不同的文化风俗习惯是非常有必要的。以上写信任务建立在教材文本的基础上，旨在引导学生思考中国特有的餐桌礼仪文化，理解其文化内涵，并学会如何用英语将这些文化介绍给外国朋友，从而发展学生跨文化沟通和传播中华文化的能力。

（六）辩论

辩论的形式可以发展学生的语言技能，培养学生的逻辑思维和批判性思维，促进多元思维。

【活动1】必修三 Unit 1 Reading One: Festivals and Celebrations

教师可以通过以下读后辩论主题渗透中国文化：

After learning the reading passage, do you think we should celebrate western festivals in China? Now the whole class will be divided into two groups holding different opinions in the debate:

The claim's opinion: We should celebrate western festivals in China.

The counter claim's opinion: We shouldn't celebrate western festivals in China.

本单元的主题语境是“人与社会”中的“不同民族文化习俗与传统节日”，语篇类型是说明文。通过该文本的学习，学生对文中所介绍的世界各地几种类型的节日有了一定的了解。通过以上辩论引导学生思考“我们是否应该在中国庆祝西方节日”这一问题，旨在让学生认识到中西方文化的差异，汲取文化精华，形成正确的价值观，即在维护中国优秀传统文化的同时，也需要以开放的思想正确看待西方的优秀文化。

【活动2】必修三 Unit 2 Reading Two: Come and Eat Here（2）

教师可以通过以下读后辩论主题渗透中国文化：

After learning the reading passage, we have known what should go into a balanced diet. Now the whole class will be divided into two groups holding different opinions in the debate:

The claim's opinion: Chinese food is healthier.

The counter claim's opinion: Western food is healthier.

本单元的主题语境是“人与自我”中的“健康的生活方式”。通过本单元两篇阅读的学习，学生对健康饮食已有一定的了解。通过让学生辩论是中国菜健康还是西方菜更健康，可以让学生更深入地了解中西方饮食文化的差异。

以上两个辩论活动都是鼓励学生学习和运用语言，开展对文化内涵的探究，特别是通过对不同观点的辩论，提高学生的鉴别能力和评判能力；同时，通过中外文化比较，培养学生的逻辑思维和批判性思维，引导学生构建多元文化视角。

五、结束语

根据《普通高中英语课程标准（2017年版）》提出的核心素养的具体要求，在高中英语教学中渗透中国文化是必不可少的，同时也能消除学生所面临的“中国文化失语症”。而在以教材为出发点的阅读教学活动中渗透中国文化的形式可以是多种多样的，不仅仅局限于本文所提的海报、续写、思维导图、课堂问答、写信和辩论这六种活动类型。笔者认为，只要教师能通过深入分析教材文本，选准切入口，设计的活动既能紧扣文本文化主题，又能提高学生相应的学科素养，就是成功渗透中国文化的阅读教学活动，也必能在一定程度上培养学生的文化意识，最终实现学科核心素养的发展目标中的“文化意识目标”。

参考文献：

［1］杜锐.高中英语教学中中国文化的渗透［J］.教学研究，2018（2）：118–124.

［2］刘妍.高中英语教学中文化意识薄弱问题管窥分析［J］.现代阅读，2013（1）：156.

［3］王初明.读后续写——提高外语学习效率的一种有效方法［J］.外语界，2012（5）：2–7.

高中英语课堂提升本土文化意识初探

——以分析《“丰”味文化》校本课程教材为例

广东省新丰县第一中学　谭玉琳

随着全球化和国际化趋势的发展，英语教学中渗透文化意识势不可当。从2008年起，教师探讨了高中英语教科书以及英语课堂上本土文化贫乏现象、文化意识薄弱现象、渗透本土文化的必要性以及渗透本土文化的有效策略等。在《普通高中英语课程标准（2017年版）》正式发行之前，越来越多的教师注重在英语课堂中提升中国本土文化意识。校本课程的开发有利于本土文化意识在英语课堂中的有效提升。本文尝试分析《“丰”味文化》校本课程教材，探讨其在高中英语课堂上提升本土文化意识的有效性，挖掘可对该校本教材改良的方面。

一、本土文化的定义和意义

本土文化是在一定地域内经一定的历史积淀下来的一种独特的审美文化，它凝结着本土人民的智慧。本土文化具有地域性、丰富性、趣味性、实践性等基本特点。

俗话说：“一方水土养一方人。”每个地方都有其特色的本土文化，从呱呱坠地开始，本土文化对一个人的成长就有着潜移默化地影响。本土文化最贴近人心，富有地域特色，能勾起学生内心的文化情愫。《普通高中英语课程标准（2017年版）》将英语教学中的文化知识界定为“中外文化知识”，扩大了高中英语教学中“文化”的范围。本土文化的渗透也是落实《普通高中英语课程标准（2017年版）》对英语学科核心素养的要求，同时兼具趣味性和知识性两大特点。

二、文化意识的定义和意义

英语学科核心素养包含语言能力、文化意识、思维品质和学习能力。其中，文化意识是指对中外文化的理解和对优秀文化的认同，是学生在全球化背景下表现出的跨文化认知、态度和行为取向。《普通高中英语课程标准（2017年版）》要求教师培养具有中国情怀、国际视野和跨文化沟通能力的社会主义建设者和接班人。文化意识的培养有助于增强学生的国家认同感和家国情怀，坚定文化自信。

《普通高中英语课程标准（2017年版）》中的文化意识要求学生在学英语的同时理解中外文化，意识到语篇反映的文化传统和社会文化现象，自觉认同优秀文化，并转化为人文修养和行为取向。用英语来学习中国本土文化，对比家乡本土文化和中国其他传统文化，意识到中国文化的意义和多样性，尊重差异，调整交际策略，进行有效沟通，最终内化为个人的文化意识和品行，树立文化自信，将家乡优秀的本土文化传播到全国各地，将中国优秀本土文化传播到全世界。通过家乡本土文化培养学生文化意识，更贴近学生生活，能更有效、快速地增强文化意识，有助于学生在学习外国文化时持有尊重理解包容的态度，进而利于形成中国情怀和国际视野。

三、《“丰”味文化》校本课程教材的内容和改进分析

《“丰”味文化》校本课程以英语学科核心素养为导向，以新丰文化为载体，以用英语推广新丰文化为目标，主要以旧人教版必修一英语教材为参照，旨在让学生巩固必修一中涉及的重点词汇和句型，培养学生在实际生活中运用英语介绍新丰的能力，同时让学生了解新丰文化，培养并增强学生的文化意识和文化自信，成为自尊、自强、自信的新丰人。

根据旧人教版必修一英语教材的内容框架，《“丰”味文化》涉及了介绍新丰概况、客家话方言、新丰自然遗产、新丰文化遗产以及新丰名人。其中，新丰自然遗产涉及鲁古河、新丰江、云髻山和秀田古树；新丰文化遗产涉及九

栋十八井、张田饼印、担丁酒和“得麻”；新丰名人涉及革命烈士李任予和救火英雄黄罗保。《“丰”味文化》校本课程内容上较丰富，包含了乡土田园、民俗风情、民间技艺、非遗文化等。学生对这些内容最为熟悉，对新丰的自然遗产和非物质文化遗产兴趣浓厚。学生不仅了解了中华传统文化之精妙，还增强了自豪感和认同感，文化意识得到了有效地提升。

与此同时，《“丰”味文化》校本课程可在以下两方面进行改良：一方面，增加学生自主探究历史渊源和精神影响课后拓展活动。黄美芳认为，本土饮食文化渗透的方式既包括用于课堂活动，引起学生兴趣，从现象渗透或从历史渗透；也包括课堂思考，引起学生探究，如文化渗透和精神渗透。《“丰”味文化》校本课程在现象渗透和文化渗透方面的内容较多，但是历史渗透和精神渗透方面的内容较少。另一方面，在英语课堂上增加体验和实践的元素。“本土文化课程的开发应当以尊重差异、丰富体验、注重实践为基本理念”。英语教师在课堂上讲解知识性的活动较多，让学生实际操作性活动较少。

虽然教师总体对英语课堂中国文化教学的认识较充分，但是教师对《普通高中英语课程标准（2017年版）》中国文化内容与要求的掌握和了解情况不容乐观，中国文化课堂教学具体实施情况堪忧，资源、课时、评价和教师素养也影响着教师开展中国文化教学。开发提升文化意识的本土文化校本课程，需要教师提升英语专业素养，不断地挖掘资源、实践和改良。在高中英语课堂提升本土文化意识，仍任重而道远。

参考文献：

［1］崔春华，杨文斌.课程情愫：学校课程发展的另类维度［M］.上海：华东师范大学出版社，2017.

［2］黄美芳.高中英语课堂中本土文化的渗透——以本土饮食文化渗透为例［J］.名师在线，2019（29）：29-30.

［3］梅明德，王蔷.普通高中英语课程标准（2017版）解读［M］.北京：高等教育出版社，2018.

［4］王晓亚.高中英语课堂中国文化教学现状调查［D］.上海：华东师范大学，2020.

关于新丰本土文化渗入初中英语课堂的必要性及如何有效渗入地探讨

新丰县第一中学实验学校　余优玲

一、新丰本土文化在我县初中英语教学中的现状

《义务教育英语课程标准（2017年版）》指出，学习一门外语能够促进人的心智发展，有助于学生认识世界的多样性，在体验中外文化的异同中形成跨文化意识，增进国际理解，弘扬爱国主义精神，形成社会责任感和创新意识，提高人文素养。然而，就笔者的观察及其与同行、学生的交流中发现，目前我县初中英语学科的教学在提供学生认识世界的多样性和中外文化的异同的体验上却是不理想的，甚至是糟糕的。它体现在哪些方面呢？具体如下：

第一，大部分初中英语教师对新丰本土文化的重视与传播意识薄弱。这导致在日常的教学中，教师只重视或过多地重视外国文化，尤其是英语文化的输入与传播，从而忽视了对本土文化的宣传与推介。

第二，在应试考试中鲜少涉及本土文化和日常英语课堂只专注于英语文化的导向下，学生普遍认为学习英语是与中国传统文化、新丰本土文化割裂的、矛盾的，学习英语是不需要本土文化作为底蕴的。

第三，教育部门在对新丰本土文化与英语的有效融合工作上目前尚是一张白纸，因此供给广大初中英语教师和学生在教学与学习中使用的资源甚少。

显然，部分学者提出的英语教学中的中国文化失语症或本土文化缺位症也存在于我县初中英语教学中。在这种模式下，广大学生对自我身份的认同感受到了严峻的挑战，在将来进行跨文化交际时，将无从表达家乡的本土文化、自

己的根源。

不过，令人欣喜的是，也有越来越多新丰教育界的有识之士认识到了这种不足，开始不断地在自身的英语教学实践中宣传与推广新丰本土文化。

二、新丰本土文化渗入初中英语课堂的必要性

（一）基于传承与发展新丰本土文化的迫切需要

新丰是千年古县，人杰地灵，素有“九山半水半分田”之称。经过长期的发展与沉淀，新丰孕育了自身独特的本土文化，诉说着新丰人民发展的故事和身份归属。这其中囊括了激励人心的红色文化，如参军第等；多姿多彩的艺术文化，如春牛舞、纸马舞等；有滋有味的饮食文化，如鸡饭、客家豆腐等。同时，《国家“十三五”时期文化发展改革规划纲要》提出，要修订和实施爱国主义教育实施纲要，丰富教育内容，创新教育载体，增强中华民族归属感、认同感、尊严感、荣誉感和命运共同体意识。而响应国家文化建设的这一号召，笔者认为首先要传播和弘扬优秀的新丰本土文化，这离不开英语学习者的化传播作。因此，基于初中英语课堂对青少年进行的新丰本土文化的推广与传承势在必行。

（二）基于为培养既传承中国优秀传统文化又兼具国际视野的新时代复合型英语人才打下坚实基础的需要

随着经济全球化的到来，我们与国际社会已不再是单向的文化吸收和输入，而是平等的双向交流。笔者认为，基于新丰本土文化的英语教学实则是为引导学生关注、传承并发展中国传统文化做好有力的铺垫，只有在讲好家乡的故事、传承家乡的本土文化的基础上，年轻的“故事家们”才能更好地讲述韶关、广东乃至中国的故事和文化精髓，祖国与世界各国平等、良性的双边交流才得以推进。

（三）基于改良课堂、提升学生学习英语积极性的需要

《义务教育英语课程标准（2017年版）》强调，现代外语教育注重语言学习的过程，强调语言学习的实践性，主张学生在语境中接触、体验和理解真实语言，并在此基础上学习和运用语言。不可否认，我们现在使用的教材是经过

专家学者审核的，几乎挑不出瑕疵。然而，教材的有些内容却脱离学生的生活实际，从而导致学生无从代入情境。但是，笔者坚信，将新丰本土文化有机地渗入初中英语课堂教学，意味着间接在课堂教学中为学生提供了源自生活的、真实的、可“触碰”的语境，学生的积极性和自信心将大大受到鼓舞和激励，学习成绩的提高自然也可期待。

那如何将新丰本土文化有效融入初中英语课堂呢？

三、将新丰本土文化有效融入初中英语课堂的途径

（一）相关部门应从宏观的角度加强对新丰本土文化的宣传与推介

一个地方的特色文化想要真正传播出去并发扬光大，离不开地方政府的宏观调控。在这一点上，政府宣传部门可以和教育部门联合，深度挖掘新丰的本土文化，并将它与英语有效地融合起来，形成线上或线下宣传海报等纸质资源，并定期发布在新丰TV、秀美新丰App上或者张贴于公交车站、各新农村建设文化广场宣传栏等。例如，在旅游方面，可以就新丰雁塔、云髻魅力小镇、参军第等制作系列宣传微短片，并使用英语讲述，配套中英文字幕；在饮食文化上，可以就各镇美食形成系列中英文宣传海报。这些看似跟课堂教学无关，实则将成为广大初中师生乃至各学段师生可以用在英语课堂的宝贵资源和素材。

（二）各学校要有意识地注重英语教学与新丰本土文化的融合，在必要的时候给予经费的支持

首先，校方通过邀请专家进行相关主题的讲座，或者组织教师外出学习与参观，让教师充分意识到英语教师既是语言的讲解者，又是文化的引导者和传播者，并让他们习得更多可操作的方法与技巧。

其次，学校教务处应该牵头骨干教师结合初中英语教学内容做好三年的新丰本土文化融入课堂的规划，开设基于新丰本土文化的英语校本课程、英语选修课等，并监督其实行与落地。

最后，学校应加强英语科组的教研、磨课，举办相关的比赛，以促进教师的积极性，如同课异构、英语教师基于新丰本土文化的演讲比赛等。同时，基

于地理、历史、生物、化学等学科等都已经配备了自己学科的教学功能室或实验室，为了更好地让本土文化渗透英语的教学，学校也应规划、打造基于本土文化教学的英语功能室，供师生使用。

（三）广大初中英语教师应提高文化自觉，重拾自信，创新教学的模式，让新丰本土文化更好地融入教学

首先，把英语课程当作文化构成物是新时代教师必须不断提升和强化的文化自觉意识。广大教师应努力做到，在教学中鼓励两种文化的互动，既要让学生学习外国文化知识，吸收和借鉴外国文化的精华，也要保持自己的民族身份，输入和输出本土文化。在备课中，教师应当深入思考教学内容融合新丰文化的可能性，同时，在条件许可的情况下，转变教学阵地，让学生亲临本土文化场景。例如，在讲到八年级下册Unit 7 What’s the highest mountain in the world?的时候，教师在各方面条件许可的情况下，可动员家长一起组织全班学生外出云髻山小镇学习，同时注重引导学生就云髻山的基本信息和当时所见所闻等尽可能使用最高级来描述，这样学生既完美地掌握了形容词、副词的最高级，也直观地受到了本土文化的感染与熏陶。

其次，教师可以利用自身的人脉或动员家长的力量联合校外的知名英语机构组织学生基于互相讲述本土文化而与该机构外教老师所在国家的学生进行互动，如作为笔友写平信、发E-mail和视频等，让学生真正参与、发现、讲述新丰本土文化和国家的故事的活动。

最后，线上教学使用的钉钉填表、问卷、云平台测试等功能，可以灵活用于收集、检测学生关于本土文化的英语知识，一举多得，物尽其用。

（四）广大初中教师应该更加注重提高自身文化修养、充实自己的课程资源库，不断搭建本土文化渗入英语课堂的金字塔

教师应当博闻强识，通过不断阅读新丰本土文化的书刊、资料和线上慕课学习等方式提升自己，切勿闭门造车，应拓宽眼界，向优秀的同行学习，“收集典型教学设计案例、典型教师授课案例、微格教学等教学素材”，让自己的教学资源库一步步充实起来。

四、结语

如果没有本土文化的指路，我们站在四通八达的路上就找不到回归故乡的道路。期待在相关部门、学校和广大初中英语教师的努力下，璀璨的新丰本土文化能早日有效地渗入初中英语课堂。

参考文献：

[1] 中华人民共和国教育部.义务教育英语课程标准［M］.北京：北京师范大学出版社，2017.

[2] 王玲端，张晓畅，王二冬，等.高职英语教学与衡水本土文化的融合［J］.衡水职业技术学院报，2017（2）：53.

[3] 曹判生.中学英语教学本土文化"失语"现象及其对策［J］.湖北教育学院学报，2007，24（3）.

[4] 杨勇.中国传统文化在英语教学中的有效渗透［J］.现代交际，2018（19）：206.

[5] 谢梅.跨文化视域下中国本土文化在高校英语课程教学中的融入［J］.高等教育，2019（3）：161.

实施方案

基于英语核心素养的高中英语本土文化教学的研究实施方案

一、本课题研究的背景

我校学生英语学习的方式多为教授型模式：课堂上教师讲授英文知识，课后辅以练习手册，并于学期末参加终结性评价。在应试教育的影响下，师生都偏重分数，较少在课堂活动中贯穿英语核心素养。当前的教学不利于应对新高考，一方面，教师充当了中心角色，不利于培养学生的思维品质和文化意识；学生害怕犯错，羞于在课堂上使用英语，导致其英语语言表达能力薄弱，跨文化交际能力未见提升。另一方面，旧版教材的知识较为陈旧，而且与学生的实际生活、所见所闻相差较远，难以激发学生的学习兴趣。相当一部分学生因月考等终结性评价分数较低且所学知识逐步加深演变成了英语学困生，失去了学习英语的兴趣。为此，基于核心素养开展高中英语本土文化教学的探究是非常有必要的。

二、课题研究的目的和意义

《普通高中英语课程标准（2017年版）》指出，“普通高中英语课程应坚持反映时代要求，根据经济社会发展新变化、科学技术进步新成果，及时更新教学内容和话语体系。课程应遵循教育教学规律和学生身心发展规律，贴近学生的思想、学习和生活实际”。由此可见，《普通高中英语课程标准（2017年版）》下的高中英语课程已经有异于《普通高中英语课程标准（实验版）》的课程，从五维目标的落实转向四个核心素养的培养，从课内的学科知识转向课外的学科拓展。因此，教学材料应该更加丰富多样，以满足不同层次学生的差异性教学，校本课程的编写和使用是《普通高中英语课程标准（2017年版）》的有益践行。

《普通高中英语课程标准（2017年版）》提出了英语学科核心素养，在此背景下，英语作为一门学习及运用英语语言的课程，强调对学生语言能力、文化意识、思维品质和学习能力的综合培养，具有工具性和人文性融合统一的特点。它注重在发展学生英语语言运用能力的过程中，帮助学生理解和鉴赏中外优秀文化，培养中国情怀，坚定文化自信。培养中国情怀，对于在较落后地区的学生来说比较抽象遥远，他们缺少与国际友人交流的机会，难以有中西方文化的碰撞体验，较难激发学生对祖国的归属感和自豪感。因此，本土特色英语教程的开发非常有必要，由学校教师调查研究后合作编写，贴近学生实际生活，立足所在地区经济文化社会，这不仅有利于接触到符合当地学情的教材，还有利于培养学生的家乡情怀和文化，进而培养学生的中国情怀和文化自信。《“丰”味英语》校本课程以英语学科核心素养为导向、以新丰本土文化为载体、以用英语推广新丰文化为目标，让学生在巩固必修一的重点词汇和句型的基础上，更多地了解新丰本土文化，培养学生在实际生活中应用英语介绍新丰的能力，并提升对本土文化和自身身份的自信，与《普通高中英语课程标准（2017年版）》的倡导和号召不谋而合。

三、课题研究的主要内容

在《普通高中英语课程标准（2017年版）》英语学科核心素养的指导下，通过《“丰”味英语》校本课程的开发和落实编写，本课题期待开发高中英语本土文化教学的方法，以实现以下三个方面的转变。

第一，通过前期对新丰本土文化的研究，开发更符合当地学生学情、更贴近学生实际生活与所见所闻的本土文化相关的教学内容，从而提高学生学习英语的兴趣，并唤起学生对所学内容的共鸣，进而提高学生学习与运用英语知识和技能的能力；通过学生对本土文化的学习，培养学生的文化意识，为学生传播中华优秀文化创作良好的条件；同时，使学生坚定文化自信，培养其家国情怀。

第二，结合多种教学方法（如情境教学法、交际法、任务教学法等），以学生为中心，改变传统教学中教师“一堂讲”的现象；通过创设与主题意义密切相关的语境，将特定主题与学生的生活建议密切关联，鼓励学生学习和运用语言，开展对语言、意义和文化内涵的探究，特别是通过对不同文化的讨论，提高学生的鉴别能力和评判能力；同时，通过中外文化比较，培养学生的逻辑思维和评判性思维，引导学生建构多元文化视角，让学生在自主学习、合作学习、探究学习等过程中提升运用英语的能力。

第三，丰富评价方式，有效结合形成性评价和终结性测试评价。其中，形成性评价强调的是过程，终结性评价强调的是结点或起点。形成性评价的关键是反馈的作用，它关注学习过程，重视非预期性结果，特别注重强化学生学习的成功之处；有助于教师了解教学得失、改进教学方法。终结性评价通常集中在学生的表现、课程实用性，学生对授课方法的态度和教师的教学风格与有效性上。单靠某一种评价方式较难全面地反映出教学成效以及学生的学习效果，所以应当将这两种评价方式有机地结合起来。科学的评价机制能激发学生的参与积极性，激励他们取得更大的进步。

四、国内外研究现状

（1）《普通高中英语课程标准（2017年版）》指出：“主题为语言学习提供主题范围或主题语境。”学生对主题意义的探究应是学生学习语言的最重要内容，直接影响学生语篇理解的程度、思维发展的水平和语言学习的成效。在课程标准所提及的三大主题语境中的“人与社会”涉及“历史、社会与文化”，而且课程标准也专门指出所有的主题语境都应包括中外文化的范畴，由此可见，本土文化在高中英语教学中的重要性。

（2）本土文化对高中英语课堂教学优化的基本方式，可以归纳为以下三点：一是合理制定高中英语教学教材中的本土文化内容，实行中外文化的比对学习；二是教师在高中英语课堂教学过程中进行本土文化的知识讲解；三是结合多媒体等教学设备，丰富高中英语课堂教学对本土文化的利用手段。

（3）根据Sandra Lee McKay的《作为国际语言的英语之教学》的引述，Cortazzi和Jin（1999）将英语教材按文化类型分为三类：①母语文化教材（Source Culture Materials），包含英语学习者自己国家的文化；②目的语文化教材（Target Culture Materials），包含英语为第一语言的国家的文化；③国际目标语文化教材（International Target Culture Materials），国际目标语指世界上所有英语国家和非英语国家中使用的各种英语。相应教材中的阅读材料也可以按主要涉及的文化不同分为本土文化、目的语文化和国际文化的阅读材料三类。

五、课题研究思路与研究方法

前期着手研究本土文化在高中英语教学中的重要性，并以英语学科核心素养为导向，开发更贴近学生实际生活与所见所闻的本土文化相关的校本课程，旨在提高学生学习英语的兴趣以及学生学习与运用英语知识和技能的能力。在之后的校本课程教学过程中，通过情境教学法、交际法、任务教学法等教学方法，培养学生的文化意识，为学生传播中国优秀文化创造良好的条件。在教学过程中创设与主题意义密切相关的语境，鼓励学生学习和运用语言，提高学生的鉴别和评判能力。同时，通过中外文化比较，培养学生的逻辑思维和评判性思维，引导学生建构多元文化视角，倡导学生在自主学习、合作学习、探究学习等过程中提升运用英语的能力。最后，通过形成性与终结性评价相结合，评价不同教学方法的成效，总结所运用到的各教学方法的利弊，从而为以后的本土化教学开发提供借鉴。

本课题旨在以最新的科研理论为依据、以探索实践中学生的动态为主线、以课堂为主的行动研究、以提高学生的英语学科核心素养为宗旨，边研究、边总结、边反思、边创新。

研究方法包括行动研究法、资料收集法、调查研究法、经验总结法。

六、完成本课题的条件分析

（1）本课题研究人员均为一线教师。

课题主持人李细娟，中学英语正高级教师，广东省特级教师，韶关市优秀英语教师，韶关市学科带头人，2014年参加了省中小学英语骨干培训，现在已经结业。2015年4月遴选为广东省中小学新一轮“百千万人才培养工程”第二批“高中文科类名教师”培养对象。2015年7月参加了首次集中培训，总体研修3年，学习了许多教育专家的讲座，有一定的理论基础和实践经验。2011年主持了一个省级课题《高中英语整体模块写作范式的研究》。2012年主持了1个市级课题《山区高中英语学困生学习兴趣的培养》。2015年主持了市级课题《运用同伴评价提升高中英语写作能力的研究》，均已结题。论文曾多次在市县教育学会获奖并在省级刊物发表多篇论文。课题组成员谭玉琳、余优伶、陈娟丽等教师，积极参加各项教科研活动，教学能力强，并在县级、市级青年教师技能竞赛中获奖，有较大的发展潜能。课题主要负责人负责课题研究的总设计、实施细则的制定、阶段性成果、结题报告等。课题组成员分别负责收集资料、问卷调查、数据统计、课题活动记录等工作。

（2）阅读了相关书籍。

例如，《外语教师如何开展小课题研究：实际操作指南》《21世纪学生发展核心素养研究》《基于学生核心素养的英语学科能力的研究》《普通高中英语课程标准（2017年版）》等有关学科素养、英语教学和课题研究的书籍。

（3）学校保证课题研究所需的全部资金。

以上都是确保课题顺利完成的有利条件。

七、课题组分工（表3-1）

表3-1　课题组分工

姓名	职称/职务	研究专长	在课题组中的分工或承担子课题
李细娟	中学英语 正高级教师	学科素养 小组合作学习	主持人、学科素养与本土文化的调查研究

续　表

姓名	职称/职务	研究专长	在课题组中的分工或承担子课题
谭玉琳	中学英语 二级教师	本土文化教学 小组合作学习	成员、学科素养与本土文化的教学案例研究
余优玲	中学英语 二级教师	本土文化教学	成员、学科素养与本土文化的教学案例研究
陈娟丽	中学英语 一级教师	本土文化教学	成员、学科素养与本土文化的教学案例研究

八、主要研究阶段

本课题利用两年的时间来完成研究，具体实施步骤分为以下三个阶段。

（一）准备阶段（2019年5—8月）

（1）成立课题组。明确课题组成员的具体分工，确定研究目标和实施步骤，组织课题申报。

（2）查找、收集相关资料。调查研究中学生英语文化素养情况，学习《普通高中英语课程标准（2017年版）》理论和相关教学理论，进行课题论证，设计研究方案。

（3）文献整理与分析。通过对相关文献资料的整理、分析与比较，探究培养学生本土文化素养的途径与方法。

（二）实施阶段（2019年9月—2021年2月）

（1）基于英语核心素养的高中英语本土文化教学的研究以英语学科核心素养为导向，以新丰本土文化为载体，以用英语推广新丰文化为目标，旨在让学生了解新丰文化，培养学生在实际生活中应用英语介绍新丰的能力。通过本课题，学生能形成批判性思维和创新性思维，并辩证地看待新丰文化以及创新性传承发扬新丰文化，通过了解新丰文化，学生能增强文化意识和文化自信，成为自尊、自强、自信的新丰人。通过课题研究，让祖国的美丽乡村文化得以弘扬。

（2）通过行动研究，调整、实施实验方案，由课题组成员从教学资源的科学性、知识性、可行性、适用性等方面对教学资源进行评价，针对问题，提出修改意见，依据课题研究方案有计划、有步骤地开展实验，所有参与教师利用收集的材料制作课件，并充分运用到课堂教学中。所有参与教师开展课堂观摩活动。

（3）进行课题10次左右的课题研讨会，进一步加强课题组成员的沟通与交流。

（三）总结阶段（2021年3—7月）

总结本课题研究，整理相关的资料、成果，完成课题研究报告，申请结题。

九、预期成果（表3-2）

表3-2　预期成果

序号	研究阶段	阶段成果名称	成果形式	负责人
1	2019年6—8月	课题研究 各环节的准备工作	课题立项材料	李细娟、谭玉琳 余优玲、陈娟丽
2	2019年9—12月	教学设计、 课例展示、中期报告	论文、教学设计汇编	李细娟、谭玉琳 余优玲、陈娟丽
3	2021年1—7月	结题报告、专题研讨会	论文	李细娟、谭玉琳 余优玲、陈娟丽

参考文献：

［1］林崇德.21世纪学生发展核心素养研究［M］.北京：北京师范大学出版社，2016.

［2］伍德沃德.如何巧妙设计英语课堂［M］.北京：外语教学与研究出版社，2009.

［3］李峰.如何利用本土文化对高中英语课堂教学进行优化［J］.都市家教·上半月，2014（8）：76.

［4］韩凤琳.牛津高中英语教材本地文化调查分析［J］.外语交流，2010（12）：35-36.

附　录

附录一 教学设计与反思模板（附表1）

附表1 教学设计与反思模板

<table>
<tr><td colspan="3">课题：Unit 3 A Taste of English Humor Reading（A Master of Nonverbal Humor）</td></tr>
<tr><td>科目: English</td><td>教学对象：高二临界班</td><td>教材版本: 人教版</td></tr>
<tr><td>提供者：陈娟丽</td><td colspan="2">单位：新丰县第一中学</td></tr>
<tr><td colspan="3">一、教学内容分析</td></tr>
<tr><td colspan="3">本单元来自人教版必修四第三单元，此文章是以“非语言幽默大师”为题，介绍了世界著名的电影演员、喜剧大师查尔斯·卓别林以及他在无声电影时代的精湛表演和辉煌成就。本节阅读课的教学重点是了解无声幽默大师——卓别林，学习阅读技巧，了解人物介绍体裁的特征，使学生学完本课后能尝试模仿本文，用英语介绍国内的著名喜剧演员，同时引导学生学习卓别林在逆境中保持乐观积极向上的态度</td></tr>
<tr><td colspan="3">二、教学目标</td></tr>
<tr><td colspan="3">知识目标：让学生掌握feel content with / badly off / worn-out / optimism等词的含义，以及难句分析、翻译的方法与技巧和人物介绍体裁的特征。
能力目标：锻炼学生总结段落大意，寻找关键词，提取细节信息和根据关键词复述文章的能力。
情感目标：让学生了解幽默的好处，并引导学生学会像卓别林一样积极面对生活中的各种困难</td></tr>
<tr><td colspan="3">三、学习者特征分析</td></tr>
<tr><td colspan="3">1.学生的基础知识水平
本班属于理科临界班，属于年级的中间水平，相对B班基础好一些，而且学生的学习积极性也比较高，多数学生都对英语有比较大的兴趣，不过语法知识基础也不太好。以其上学期期末成绩为例：在及格以上的只有3人，占了5.5%，没有学生达到优秀以上，40分以下的有5人，占了9.3%。
2.学生的学习能力
多数学生有较强的学习能力，但仍没有养成很好的自主学习习惯，还是经常只做教师要求的作业，较少学生能自主进行预习、复习，所以导致所学知识无法及时巩固，基础依然较难得到提高。但是学生逐渐愿意在英语上多花时间，上课氛围也比较活跃积极</td></tr>
<tr><td colspan="3">四、教学策略选择与设计</td></tr>
<tr><td colspan="3">本节课各教学环节都围绕以上教学目标以及学情而设，运用Group work / discussion / Task-driven method等教学策略，力求最大限度地实现这些目标。具体的教学设想如下：</td></tr>
</table>

续 表

四、教学策略选择与设计		
第一部分的引入，引导学生联想他们熟悉的中国喜剧演员，为后面介绍自己喜爱的中国喜剧演员活动做铺垫，并引出本文的主角——杰出的幽默大师卓别林，让学生熟悉卓别林非语言幽默的展示方式。第二部分是扫除障碍，通过单词、短语复习，以及检测学生预习的长难句翻译，为学生扫除下面阅读环节可能遇到的障碍，降低阅读难度。第三部分是通过快速阅读，锻炼学生快速获取段落大意的技巧。第四部分是通过scanning，锻炼学生找读细节信息的能力，并通过视频让学生更直观地感受卓别林的幽默。第五部分是引导学生认识并学习卓别林积极乐观的精神。第六部分是通过一个简单的思维导图，引导学生回顾本节课所学的卓别林相关信息。 本班一直以来都实行小组竞争性教学，效果甚好，本节课很多练习都提供给各小组抢答以及轮流回答，一是能激发学生之间的良性竞争、提高学生的合作精神与团队意识，二是能活跃课堂气氛		
五、教学重点及难点		
教学重点： 1.了解卓别林的生平以及其幽默特征。 2.锻炼总结段落大意、寻找关键词、提取细节信息和根据关键词复述文章的能力。 教学难点：锻炼学生总结段落大意、寻找关键词、提取细节信息、绘制思维导图和根据思维导图复述文章的能力		
六、教学过程		
教师活动	学生活动	设计意图
1.Teacher asks students "Can you name any famous Chinese comedy actors?", shows some examples after students' sharing; asks students "Do you know any famous English humorists?" 2.Teacher explains the concept of humor and asks students the differences between verbal humor and nonverbal humor	1.Students put hands to name some famous Chinese comedy actors and English humorists they know; Students explain the differences between verbal humor and nonverbal humor. 2.The whole class is divided into 8 groups. In the whole class, all groups should race to gain as many points as they can	引导学生联想他们熟悉的中国喜剧演员，再引到外国喜剧演员，点出本课主角，为后面介绍自己喜爱的中国喜剧演员活动做铺垫；帮助学生理解什么是幽默，引起学生阅读的兴趣，为阅读储备相关背景知识
1.Teacher asks the whole class to translate the words and phrases into Chinese	1.Students read the words and phrases, and say out their Chinese meanings	帮助学生在阅读前扫清部分单词与难句障碍，降低阅读难度

续 表

六、教学过程		
教师活动	学生活动	设计意图
2.Teacher asks four students randomly to translate the difficult sentences which were assigned as homework the day before, and helps students to analyze the sentence structure	2.Students translate the sentences into Chinese.（If their answers are correct, their respective groups can gain 2 points per time.） 3.Students read the sentences together	
Teacher asks students to match the main idea of each paragraph and gives students some hints if necessary	Students race to be the first one to match the main idea and try to find out the keywords of each main idea.（If their answers are correct, their respective groups can gain 1 point per time.）	通过快速阅读，让学生掌握快速获取段落大意的技巧
Teacher explains how to scan the text and what should be paid attention to while scanning. Teacher checks the answers with students. Teacher plays the video	1.Students scan the text paragraph by paragraph and gain the required information.（Students may raise their hands to answer if they know the answers. They can get 1 point per blank.） 2.Students work in groups to put the events of the 4th paragraph in order, and the quickest two groups go to the backboard to write their answers. 3.Students enjoy the short video of Chaplin eating shoes	1.让学生找读课文，获取卓别林个人信息资料； 2.让学生仔细阅读文章，提取细节信息； 3.通过视频让学生更直观地感受卓别林的幽默
Teacher asks students what they can learn from Chaplin	Students discuss it in groups and 2 groups may share the result	引导学生认识并学习卓别林积极乐观的精神
Teacher leads students to summarize the information about Chaplin according to the mind map	Students follow teacher's guidance to summarize the information about Chaplin according to the mind map	通过一个简单的思维导图，引导学生回顾本节课所学的卓别林的相关信息

续 表

<table>
<tr><td colspan="3">六、教学过程</td></tr>
<tr><td>教师活动</td><td>学生活动</td><td>设计意图</td></tr>
<tr><td>The teacher explains the homework to students</td><td>1.Retell the text according to the mind map drawn in the last part, and write it down.
2.Use a mind map to introduce one of your favorite Chinese comedy actors</td><td>1.通过重温上一环节的思维导图，复述课文，并写出来，可锻炼学生总结的能力；
2.通过上一个作业，再次熟悉人物介绍的要素并让学生模仿介绍他们自己喜爱的中国喜剧演员，借此让学生对比中外幽默，增强他们的本土文化情怀</td></tr>
<tr><td colspan="3">七、教学评价设计</td></tr>
</table>

The things I did	Evaluation
I played an active role in this class	5 4 3 2 1
I expressed myself in English very well	5 4 3 2 1
I followed my teacher well and took some necessary notes	5 4 3 2 1
I have learned how to scan the text and find out the main idea of the text	5 4 3 2 1
I have learned how to summarize the main ideas	5 4 3 2 1
TOTAL SCORES	
20 ~ 25：Excellent 15 ~ 19：Very good 10 ~ 14：Good 5 ~ 9：Just so so 1 ~ 4：Need to improve	

续 表

八、板书设计（本节课的主板书）
如板书中含有特殊符号、图片等内容，为方便展示，可将板书以附件或图片形式上传
A Master of Nonverbal Humor Para 1 Chaplin's Effect Para 2 Childhood Para 3 The Little Tramp Para 4 Example Para 5 Achievements 计分板： G1 G5 G2 G6 G3 G7 G4 G8 学生成果展示： （1） （2）
九、教学反思
教师可以从如下角度进行反思（不少于200字）： （1）优点。 准备充分，汇报课的前一天曾在另一个班级磨课，并将发现的问题及时解决； 教学环节设计合理，环环相扣，尤其是第二部分的“扫除障碍”环节为之后的教学环节做了铺垫，能提高学生之后的学习效率； 板书字体大小适中，字迹清晰、有条理，板块分布得当； PPT设计比较花心思，字体明了、有条理，又不会过于花哨，不会过于分散学生的注意力； 在学生完成任务的时候，教师先引导学生回顾之前所学过的技巧，或给予一定的提示，便于学生更好、更快地完成任务； 在学完课文之后，引导学生进行感情升华，使学生从中学会积极面对困难等态度， 在作业部分通过思维导图+关键词，引导学生回顾本节课所学内容，并通过写作和模仿写作的输入方式检验自己本节课的学习效果； 第一环节的引入为最后作业做铺垫，引导学生对比中外幽默，增强他们的本土文化情怀。 （2）不足之处。 PPT上的教学目标一页播放得太快，应该让学生更加明确本节课他们所要掌握的内容与能力； 本节课的scanning部分，练习形式较为单一； 本节课的容量相对较大，虽然学生整节课下来掌握程度不错，但不够深入； 留给学生提问的时间较少

续 表

九、教学反思
（3）教学感悟。 通过本节汇报课，本人获益良多。各位教师的点评都很中肯到位，给予我很多有建设性的建议。针对本节汇报课所反映出来的优缺点，我今后将从以下几方面继续努力改进： ① 继续发扬本节汇报课上所反映出来的优点； ② 多听各位老教师的课，尤其是师父的课，综合各位教师的经验与建议，将其内化为自己的教学风格；多向师父以及其他经验丰富的教师请教； ③ 认真备好每节课，备好学情，做到有的放矢地设置每个教学环节，并把控好每个环节的用时，逐渐提高对课堂时间的把控能力，力求在课堂有限的时间内最大限度地完成教学目标； ④阅读课全文讲完，一节课的容量较大，以后可以考虑分两节课讲，每节课侧重讲其中一些段落，以便讨论其中更深层次的内容与内涵等

附录二 英语调查问卷（附表2）

《英语核心素养下的本土文化教学》学生课堂学习评价表

School ____________ Class ________

Name ____________ Grade ______

Date ____________ Student NO. ____________

附表2 英语调查问卷表

项目	具体表现	细则	个人评价	同学评价	教师评价
语言能力	能巩固旧人教版必修一英语课本中的重点词汇、句型等	能（4～5分） 基本能（2～3分） 不能（<1分）			
	能理解各单元多模态语篇传递的关于新丰文化的内容，辨识语篇结构和意图，根据上下文推断要义				
	能在日常生活中使用英语介绍新丰文化，并表达自己对新丰文化的看法				
	能分析不同体裁英语作文并进行写作，使用得体的语言表达自己的观点				
文化意识	能意识到新丰县不同镇区的文化差异，并做出自己的评价	能（4～5分） 基本能（2～3分） 不能（<1分）			
	能与来自新丰县不同镇区的同学有效地进行跨文化沟通交流				
	能在深入认识新丰文化后认同新丰文化，更加自尊、自强、自信				
思维品质	能观察到身边的新丰文化，比较新丰县各镇区文化的异同	能（4～5分） 基本能（2～3分） 不能（<1分）			
	能分析语篇，厘清文本内在关系，推断出语言表层结构下的深层意思，归纳文章大意				

续 表

项目	具体表现	细则	个人评价	同学评价	教师评价
思维品质	能对新丰文化提出疑问并积极求证，认识到新丰文化的优劣，扬长避短，既不全盘接收，也不全盘否定	能（4～5分） 基本能（2～3分） 不能（<1分）			
	能提出在当今信息时代弘扬新丰文化的新见解和新方法				
学习能力	对学习本土文化的英语课堂感兴趣，能主动使用英语参与课堂，勤于思考，并写出自己的成果	能（4～5分） 基本能（2～3分） 不能（<1分）			
	能通过调查、实践、查阅等途径获取最新的知识和信息，并整合信息完成学习任务				
	能通过自主学习、合作学习、探究学习等方式，认真听取他人意见并询问，积极表达自己的意见，多角度地解读和评判多元新丰文化现象				
个人评价总得分					
同学评价总得分					
教师评价总得分					
最终总得分					

说明：1.本评价表针对学生课堂表现情况做评价，总分为100分，评价具体方面共20项，每项得分最高5分，最终总得分按自评、同学评和教师评，分数5∶2∶3的比例取均值。

2. 本评价表从英语学科核心素养的4个方面进行评价，主要参考《普通高中英语课程标准（2017解读版）》中第56、63、72、73、80页的内容。

新丰一中"丰"味英语校本课程学生问卷调查表

——"丰"味英语教材编写组

同学：

你好！为了使校本课程的教学更为规范、高效，切实起到发展学生个性的作用，编写组想了解一下本学期你所选的校本课程的教学等情况。请对照实际情况做出判断，在相应的项目后的括号里填上字母。相信有了你的合作，我们校本课程的设计会越来越科学，教学质量也会不断提高。

你选的校本课程是：__________ 开课的教师是：__________

一、关于校本课程的内容方面

1. 校本课程内容编排科学合理、结构清晰，与学生水平相适应。（　　）

A. 非常满意　　B. 比较满意

C. 一般　　D. 不满意

2. 校本课程有机结合了新丰本土文化和高一必修1的重难点词汇和表达。（　　）

A. 非常满意　　B. 比较满意

C. 一般　　D. 不满意

3. 校本课程具有完整的系列性，配有相应的听说读写看的内容。（　　）

A. 非常满意　　B. 比较满意

C. 一般　　D. 不满意

4. 校本课程生动呈现了新丰的本土文化，激起了我的学习兴趣。（　　）

A. 非常满意　　B. 比较满意

C. 一般　　D. 不满意

5. 校本课程包含了有规划的学习检测和有依据性的成绩评定。（　　）

A. 非常满意　　B. 比较满意

C. 一般　　D. 不满意

二、关于校本课程的课堂教学方面

6. 教师教学设计完整，备课认真充分，课堂重难点突出。（　　）

A. 非常满意　　B. 比较满意

C. 一般　　D. 不满意

7. 教师的教学充分体现学生的主体地位，注重引导学生自主探究，提供学生主动参与课堂的机会。（　　）

A. 非常满意　　B. 比较满意

C. 一般　　D. 不满意

8. 教师上课热情投入、仪容仪态良好，能充分掌控课堂。（　　）

A. 非常满意　　B. 比较满意

C. 一般　　D. 不满意

9. 教师对他所教的这门课有一定的研究，能胜任本课程的教学。（　　）

A. 非常满意　　B. 比较满意

C. 一般　　D. 不满意

10. 通过教师的讲解，我每一堂课都有相应的收获。（　　）

A. 非常满意　　B. 比较满意

C. 一般　　D. 不满意

三、对这位教师、这门课程你还有什么好的建议，请写在下面

____

____

____

____

____

____

____

____

新丰中学学生对新丰本土文化的了解调查问卷

尊敬的同学：

您好!“丰味”文化课题组正在做一项关于我县中学生对新丰本土文化的了解的问卷调查，以初步掌握学生对新丰本土文化的认知，促进新丰本土文化与初高中英语课堂的有机融合，最终使本土文化持续、健康发展。本次问卷调查不记名，仅为课题研究所用，请您如实选择或直接填写。感谢您的参与。

一、单选题

1. 您认为自己了解新丰本土文化吗？（　　）

A. 了解很深　　B. 知道一点

C. 不了解　　D. 漠不关心

2. 您身边的亲人、同学、朋友对新丰本土文化了解吗？（　　）

A. 了解很深　　B. 知道一点

C. 不了解　　D. 漠不关心

3. 您认为中小学生有必要学习新丰本土文化吗？（　　）

A. 很有必要　　B. 有必要

C. 没必要　　D. 无所谓

4.您能简单地使用英语对外国友人推介新丰本土文化吗？（　　）

A. 完全没有问题　　B. 没有问题

C. 有一点问题　　D. 不可以

二、多选题

5.您平日里接触新丰本土文化的途径有哪些？（　　）

A. 课堂　　B. 长辈讲述

C. 网络媒介　　D. 各类书籍

E. 自行实地探访

6.在上述接触新丰本土文化的途径中，给您留下最深刻印象的前三种途径是？（　　）

A. 课堂　　B. 长辈讲述

C. 网络媒介　　D. 各类书籍

E. 自行实地探访

7.您对下列哪些本土文化比较感兴趣或者了解？（　　）

A. 手工艺（如张田饼印）　　B. 文学艺术（如纸马舞、春牛舞等）

C. 饮食文化　　D. 当地民俗（如担丁酒等）

E. 自然风景景观文化　　F. 烈士英雄（如李任予等）

8.对于当代中学生，您觉得以下哪种方法能快速地提升您对新丰本土文化的认识？请排序。（　　）

A. 自身多与新丰本土文化接触

B. 自觉形成保护新丰本土文化的意识

C. 政府应当采取措施保护新丰本土文化

D. 学校加强对学生进行新丰本土文化的熏陶

E. 其他

9.您认为把新丰本土文化融入初高中课堂会带来哪些改变？（　　）

A. 使初高中英语课堂变得更贴近生活、生动

B. 学生对新丰本土文化的认知程度得以提高

C. 学生对身份的认同感更加强烈

D. 学生使用英语讲好新丰故事、推介新丰本土文化的能力大大提高

三、简答题

10. 若将新丰本土文化与初高中英语课堂有机融合，您最希望看到一个怎么样的课堂？请简单列出二点。

____

____

____

附录三 研讨相关照片